REFLECTING
HIM

REFLECTING HIM

LIVING FOR JESUS AND LOVING IT

CARLA MCDOUGAL

© 2010 by Carla McDougal. All rights reserved.

WinePress Publishing (PO Box 428, Enumclaw, WA 98022) functions only as book publisher. As such, the ultimate design, content, editorial accuracy, and views expressed or implied in this work are those of the author.

No part of this publication may be reproduced, stored in a retrieval system, or transmitted in any way by any means—electronic, mechanical, photocopy, recording, or otherwise—without the prior permission of the copyright holder, except as provided by USA copyright law.

Unless otherwise noted, all Scripture references are taken from the *Holy Bible, New International Version*®*, NIV*®. Copyright © 1973, 1978, 1984 by Biblica, Inc.™ Used by permission of Zondervan. All rights reserved worldwide. WWW.ZONDERVAN.COM

Scripture references marked NKJV are taken from the *New King James Version*. Copyright © 1982 by Thomas Nelson, Inc. Used by permission. All rights reserved.

Hebrew/Greek definitions are from *Strong's Concordance of the Bible*.

ISBN 13: 978-1-60615-033-7
ISBN 10: 1-60615-033-2
Library of Congress Catalog Card Number: 2009941340

CONTENTS

Acknowledgments vii
Introduction ix

Week 1: Reflections in Life: Images in the Mirror 1

Week 2: Created for God, by God: Like Clay in the Hands of the Potter 5
    Day 1: The Touch of the Potter 9
    Day 2: The Lump of Clay 13
    Day 3: The Spinning of the Wheel 17
    Day 4: The Uniqueness of Imperfections 23
    Day 5: The Firing Process 27

Week 3: Senses of the Soul: The Touch, Aroma, Taste, Sight, and Sound of Jesus 33
    Day 1: Open the Eyes of My Soul 35
    Day 2: A Touch to the Soul 41
    Day 3: The Taste of Jesus 45
    Day 4: The Aroma of Christ 51
    Day 5: Ears to Hear 55

Week 4: The Power Source: The Father, the Son, and the Holy Spirit 61
    Day 1: The Dawning Light 63
    Day 2: Here Comes the Son! 67
    Day 3: The Sun-Earth Connection 71
    Day 4: The Sun Link 75
    Day 5: Light Up My Life! 79

Week 5: Prayer from the Inside Out: The Holy Spirit Initiates Prayer 83
    Day 1: The Closet 85
    Day 2: The Bedroom 89
    Day 3: The Kitchen 93
    Day 4: The Living Room 97
    Day 5: The Windows 101

Week 6: Prayer Fuels Faith: Prayer Energizes Faith into Action 105
    Day 1: Trusting the Unseen 107
    Day 2: Preparing the Heart 111

    Day 3: Diggin' In! 117
    Day 4: Move into Action! 121
    Day 5: The Outcome 125

Week 7: The Control Syndrome: Consequences of Running Ahead 129
    Day 1: Soil of the Soul 131
    Day 2: The Waiting Time 135
    Days 3 and 4: Garden Invasions—Weeds and Pests 139
    Day 5: Companion Planting 145

Week 8: Roadblocks Ahead: Caution—Diversions Along the Way 149
    Day 1: Forks in the Road 151
    Day 2: Detours in Life 155
    Day 3: The Work Zone 159
    Day 4: Watch for Potholes 163
    Day 5: Caution: Slow Traffic Ahead! 167

Week 9: Fit for Jesus: Get Up! Get Out! Get Going! 171
    Day 1: Training for the Prize 173
    Day 2: Enduring the Race 177
    Day 3: Strength Training 181
    Day 4: Team Building 185
    Day 5: Final Instructions 189

Week 10: So . . . Reflect Him: Love God, Live for Jesus, Breathe in the Holy Spirit 193

Bibliography 199
Endnotes 201

Leader's Guide and **Teaching Materials** for *Reflecting Him* are available to download online at
www.reflectivelifeministries.org

ACKNOWLEDGMENTS

Reflecting Him is a true example of the body of Christ working together to accomplish His purposes. This was a team effort, and I thank God for fitting all the pieces together. I would like to begin by praising my Lord and Savior, Jesus Christ. Without Him this Bible study would be filled with blank pages. He is the reason for every word in this book. I smile as I recall the many hours I spent with Him. In my humbleness, God has confirmed this scripture: "My grace is sufficient for you, for my power is made perfect in weakness" (2 Cor. 12:9). Yes, sister, my weakness!

A big "thank you" goes to my family for their love and support. My husband, Fred, served as my encourager through the times of fear. When doubts entered my mind, he spurred me forward toward the finish line. He and our four children, Luke, Jake, Tate, and Carly Jo, prayed for this project since the moment it began back in May of 2008. I thank my parents, Carl and Glenda Williams, for believing in this call upon my life. I love each of you dearly!

What would I have done without Kitty Self? Through God's perfect timing she partnered with me as my editor, and we both learned so much. Her willingness to teach and coach me through these months has blessed me beyond words. Thank you, Kitty, for sticking with me—you are a blessing!

There are not enough words to thank those who donated funds for this project. Without them, this Bible study would still be words on my computer. Thank you for partnering with me.

I am grateful for the people who helped along the way. Cynthia Bonner shared her expert advice for Week 2, "The Pottery Process." Claire Hardin, a registered nurse, supported me through Week 3, "Senses of the Soul." Carl Williams gave words of wisdom for Week 4, "The Power Source." I send a big kiss to my husband, Fred, for his role as our tour guide for Week 6, "Prayer Fuels Faith." Ross McCall assisted with advice on Week 8, "Roadblocks Ahead." Dr. Kem Oberholtzer Th.M., Ph.D., a graduate from Dallas Theological Seminary with a Doctor in Theology in Biblical Literature, made sure I stayed on track from a biblical prospective. Melinda Trawick used her creative gifts and talents in photography (www.melindatrawick.com) to create the incredible photo for the cover. Anna DeBord, a graduate from Pepperdine University in Graphic Design, blessed us with the graphics within the chapters and cover ideas. Wow, what a team!

REFLECTING HIM

Finally, the remarkable people on the Reflective Life Ministries' team perform as a "dream team." Their giving hearts and loving spirits continually compel RLM forward as a ministry sold out to Jesus. Thanks to each of you who poured out your hearts through prayer and fasting. Thank you for standing in the gap!

Janice Drees
Carole Weldon - Jack
Ann Foster - Tom
Ceelina Dixon
Laura
Roxanne
Theda
Sande

INTRODUCTION

The first week of *Reflecting Him* unfolded while my husband and I cruised in Glacier Bay, Alaska. My heart filled with awe at the power of the gigantic masses of ice. For a while, I seemed to be watching a television documentary. But reality sank in when I heard a sound like roaring thunder. All of a sudden, a small section of ice plummeted down the fringe of the glacier! I watched with anticipation as a more substantial segment also tumbled from the top and a mountain of ice plunged into the sea. This powerful noise echoed throughout the bay as if to say, "I am glacier; hear me roar!"

At this point, one of God's truths became clear to me. In life, we experience a variety of intense pressures—financial, physical, emotional, relational, and more. As these intensify, we feel a cold, heavy burden begin to settle upon us, as if to freeze us in our tracks. But God, in His perfect timing, is always there to remove the weight of the world. He has the power to bring down the ice-cold walls, freeing us from life's pressures. It is so much fun to open our eyes to God's daily life lessons!

This glacier experience confirmed God's call for me to write this Bible study. My heart's desire is to help others catch a glimpse of Jesus as He works in their lives, allowing each of us to reflect Him as we relate to one another.

You might be asking yourself why you need another Bible study or how this study is different from others. The answer lies in the fact, as someone said, that life is so *daily*. It can become routine. When we first become Christians, we are eager to please God. We yearn to live a life that mirrors Jesus' teachings and glorifies Him. As time passes, it often becomes difficult to keep this fire burning. As a result, we need practical reminders to help us walk in the Spirit and not in the flesh. I pray this study encourages you to find those day-to-day moments that God uses to illuminate His teachings.

Think about the pictures, scenes, objects, and events depicted in Scripture to communicate truth. In addition to parables, Jesus illustrated His teaching with things around him—fishing nets, a farmer, sheep. This gave His listeners a physical application for the lesson. God still uses this method to teach us today. *Reflecting Him* will motivate you to look for Jesus in your everyday experiences. The more you ask the Holy Spirit to reveal these applications, the more you will recognize His hand in your daily life. Get ready for some fun moments as God reveals His truths to you. I pray an excitement is brewing within your heart as you begin your journey through *Reflecting Him*.

This study consists of ten weeks (chapters) designed to lead you into a deeper, more intimate walk with Jesus. Each week is divided into five days (lessons), supporting the central theme for the week. Each daily lesson includes these elements:

- Introduction to the topic for the day
- Scripture Excavation—Digging into certain scriptures
- Hidden Treasures—Connecting the week's theme with the designated scriptures
- Celebrating Treasured Gifts—Applying Jesus' teachings to your life and taking time to praise God
- Reflection Pause—Connecting the weekly topic with God's Word and drawing near to the Lord through your everyday experiences

Let's not wait another minute for the journey to begin!

WEEK 1

REFLECTIONS IN LIFE: IMAGES IN THE MIRROR

And we, who with unveiled faces all reflect the Lord's glory, are being transformed into his likeness with ever-increasing glory, which comes from the Lord, who is the Spirit.
—2 Corinthians 3:18

God, help! What is wrong with me? Why do I feel this way? On the outside everything appeared in order—spiritual life, marriage, children, friends, health. Yet inside, the feeling of death simmered. Not a physical death, but a living death. My joy slowly faded into the darkness. *But I am a Christian. I love Jesus. How can I have these thoughts?* No one knew. I put on a facemask as part of my daily attire. That superficial smile looked very real on this thirty-three-year-old woman!

Can't he see what he is doing to me? He needs to be more sensitive! My marriage teetered back and forth. Laughter withered away. To my way of thinking, our problems existed because of my husband. I thought we needed marriage counseling.

REFLECTING HIM

It is two A.M. These clothes must be folded. The dishes need washing. Look at these toys all over the floor. I can't go to sleep until everything is done! I can't halt my life! I must keep going. Mothering four young children required love, discipline, and steadfastness. I knew they needed me. I turned off the light and curled up in the corner of the playroom. Tears poured from my eyes. *God, help!* This is all I prayed, and all God wanted—my surrendered heart.

Depression? Are you sure? I don't even take naps during the day. In fact, I hardly sleep at all. Christians don't have depression problems. Joy is part of our job description! Yes, I believed the lie that Christians couldn't be depressed. Are you ready for this? I believed a Christian who struggled with depression just needed a stronger relationship with Jesus. There wasn't a book or a lecture that could change my opinion. Little did I know that God needed to teach me a thing or two about humility and compassion! So in His tender way He allowed me to experience firsthand this dreaded thing called "depression." He walked me through each step, teaching me to trust Him. In time I realized I couldn't blame anyone for my condition—not my family, not God. The Lord used the doctors and medicines to bring physical healing. In turn, this healing allowed me to grow deeper in my walk with the Lord. As a result, I come before you a humble woman. I thank God for bringing me through my depression. Knowing where I used to be in my life and where I am today brings tears to my eyes. As I reflect on this experience, I realize that God embedded His promise in my heart. Deuteronomy 31:6 says, "He will never leave you nor forsake you." Amen!

With a shout of joy I can say that God rescued me from the pit of depression at age thirty-five. I asked the Lord to use my past for His glory. I desired to be a light in the darkness for others experiencing this same hopelessness. I prayed for the Holy Spirit to reveal to me those who needed prayer. I found the more I prayed, the more I reflected Jesus. I craved to know Him, read His Word, praise His name, and worship Him!

Never in a million years did I think God would use me to serve Him. No way, not me! I mean, look at my past. However, about five years after my battle with depression, I experienced a stirring within my heart. In my quiet times with God, I sensed Him telling me to share my story—not with one woman, but with groups of women. For about a year I didn't share this with anyone, not even my husband. Why? Fear gripped me. Over and over I talked with God about this pull on my heart. I shared my weaknesses with Him, as if He didn't know them already. I heard Him whisper, "*When you are weak, I am strong.*" Then I reminded him of my past experiences. He answered, "*All for My glory.*" Finally, I knew this next question would change His mind: "God, what about my dyslexia? I can't read the Bible in front of people." His response: "*I know. I will do it for you, just as I helped Moses speak to crowds of people.*" At that moment I realized that when God says to surrender it *all*, He means everything. And we need to expect the unexpected!

With my body trembling, I finally shared all of these thoughts and prayers with my man. I honestly believed he would advise me against moving forward. But to my surprise he supported God's call for me to minister to women. Still doubting, however, I pleaded with God to give me an outward sign. You know, like a burning bush! A couple of weeks later I mentioned my need for prayer to some of my girlfriends. Before I could explain why, one of them said she knew the request. These words flowed from her lips: "Carla, God is calling you to be a Christian women's speaker."

I almost fell out of my chair as I said, "How did you know?"

My sweet friend next to her said, "For the past five years, I prayed God would call you into this ministry." The Holy Spirit's sweet and tender presence immediately penetrated each of our souls. A shared memory . . . the power of God . . . a moment to behold!

At that point, in the quiet of my heart, I realized that God has a plan for each of us. He writes the pages of our life stories, all for His glory. All He asks is for us to give Him access to do His will in our lives. Doubt flooded my mind as fear emerged. Again, these same words flowed from my mouth: "God, help!" This is all I prayed, and all God wanted—my surrendered heart!

God, you have to be joking! Write a Bible study? Not me! Again, I resisted God's call. I shared with Him why, in my opinion, He needed a different vessel for this project. *I am not a writer. You must mean someone else. Remember my reading disability?* I started debating with God again. Then one day I read a verse that opened the

REFLECTIONS IN LIFE: IMAGES IN THE MIRROR

curtain to a play in my heart. Before me on stage God sang these words: "And we, who with unveiled faces all reflect the Lord's glory, are being transformed into his likeness with ever-increasing glory, which comes from the Lord, who is the Spirit" (2 Cor. 3:18). Applauding, as in an audience, I shouted, *God, help!* This is all I prayed, and all God wanted—my surrendered heart!

With hands lifted high and shouts of praise in my heart—I am committed to *Reflecting Him*! I desire to live my life sold out to Jesus. It humbles me to think of all He has done, is doing, and will do. He rescued me from the pit of despair and saved me from the trenches of darkness. Jesus is the Way, the Truth, and the Life! I am so excited about *Living for Jesus and Loving It!*

I am thrilled you are joining me in this ten-week journey. God has so much in store for us. Each week we will focus on a different aspect of life and compare it to a spiritual truth. Here is a sample of the questions we will consider over the next few weeks:

- How does the pottery process resemble your spiritual life?
- How can God use our five senses to teach us about Jesus?
- What spiritual truths can we gain from studying the sun-earth connection?
- What can God teach us about prayer as we walk through each room of the house?
- How can pumping gas into a car remind us of faith?
- Is working in your garden or flowerbed enjoyable? (You will love this powerful analogy!)
- How can road construction teach you to live daily for Jesus?
- Exercise is essential for our physical bodies. Why is spiritual exercise vital for a believer?

Before you move into this study, spend a few minutes in prayer. Then answer these questions, being truthful and honest. Read 2 Corinthians 3:18. Reflect, listen, and respond.

Why am I committing to this study for the next ten weeks?

_____

_____

If a friend asked you about your relationship with Jesus, how would you answer his or her question? In other words, where are you in your walk with the Lord?

_____

_____

In the last week of the study you are asked to reread what you wrote in Week 1. This is a key component to any Bible study—the review. Examining your spiritual life at the beginning of the study will help you to observe changes at the end of the study. What do you desire your spiritual walk to be at the end of these ten weeks?

_____

_____

What comes to mind when you hear the word "reflection?" Read 1 Corinthians 13:11–13. What does Paul mean when he talks about a poor reflection?

_____

_____

REFLECTING HIM

Reflecting Him is what God wants from His children—for us be more like Jesus, with a desire to love Him with all our hearts, souls, and minds. Are you committed to *Reflecting Him*? Write your commitment. Get excited as you begin *Living for Jesus and Loving It!*

_____

_____

Reflecting Him Group Discussion

God placed you in this group for a reason. Take note of who is on this journey with you. Reflect. Breathe in the moment. Discuss the following:

- Why has God placed you together to study His Word for the next ten weeks?
- Be real! Take off the masks and get real with one another. All it takes is one woman to start talking and get the ball rolling.
- Go through the questions in Week 1. This is a great way to connect with the group.
- Pray together. Ask the Lord to connect all of you in a tender and sweet way.

Reflection Pause

One look in the mirror can sometimes send me spinning out of control. Ever experienced one of those moments? Everything is going as planned. You're feeling a sense of accomplishment. And then you casually glance in the mirror.

I left the house early one morning to run some errands and then help at my daughter's elementary school. Halfway through the day, I needed to use the restroom. As I walked in, I looked over at the mirror and gasped. Then I started talking to myself out loud, "I can't believe this! How could I forget to zip up my pants? It is part of getting dressed. My life is just too busy!" Looking straight in the mirror, I let myself have it. My mind started backtracking to everywhere I'd been that morning. All of a sudden, a woman opened one of the stall doors and tiptoed to the sink. She never looked at me. A thick silence pervaded the bathroom. Red-faced and embarrassed, I smiled. Without a word, she turned, dried her hands, and walked out the door.

If I had taken a closer look in the mirror that morning, I never would have experienced this embarrassment. Like looking in the mirror, we need to keep our eyes on Jesus so that we become a reflection of Him. "And we, who with unveiled faces all reflect the Lord's glory, are being transformed into his likeness with ever-increasing glory, which comes from the Lord, who is the Spirit" (2 Cor. 3:18). Amen!

Reflecting Him Team List

Name	Phone	E-mail

WEEK 2

CREATED FOR GOD, BY GOD: LIKE CLAY IN THE HANDS OF THE POTTER

We are the clay, you are the potter; we are all the work of your hand.

—Isaiah 64:8

Why did God create man? Theologians and scholars have debated this for centuries. What were God's reasons for creating a being equipped not only with a physical body but also a mind, soul, reasoning ability, conscience, spirit, and free will? Why would God, who is perfect and flawless, mold a man from the dust of the earth and place him in a perfect paradise, knowing all along that man would fall into sin? Digging into God's Word and asking the Holy Spirit to reveal the hidden treasures of truth are imperative to your walk with our Lord Jesus Christ.

In Genesis 1:27, we read, "God created man in his own image; in the image of God he created him; male and female he created them." God blessed man, instructed him to multiply, and gave him authority on earth to rule over every living thing. God entrusted man with the power to supervise things on this earth. But is this the only reason God created man—to manage His property and possessions? With a big shout, I say "no"! We must go a little farther in the Bible. Genesis 1:31 tells us that after God created the things on the sixth day of creation, "God saw all that he had made, and it was *very* good" (emphasis mine). It is interesting to note that after the other days of creation God said, "It was good," but after the creation of man His statement was, "It was *very* good." The Hebrew word here for *good* is *towb*, which means "to be good, pleasing, joyful, beneficial, pleasant, favorable, happy, or right."[1] In other words, "very good" actually means God was exceedingly pleased with His creation of man. Can't you hear the love flowing from His lips?

Now we're getting somewhere! God loves each one of His creations independently and personally! Is this the whole reason for the formation of mankind? Look at 1 John 4:19, "We love because He first loved us." Think about that for a moment—God loves each one of us first, *before* we know Him. He designs each person in a specific way to accomplish His purposes and to further His kingdom. He is the Master Designer with a master plan. Personally, I would like to see an outline of my life with all of the blanks filled in, wouldn't you? Have fun this week as you discover that you were created for God, by God!

The Pottery Process

Have you ever dreamed of creating a piece of handmade pottery? Let's delve into the entire pottery process. This week we analyze the potter's necessary skills, the clay's individual characteristics, the wheel's purpose, the importance of removing the imperfections in each vessel, and the firing process's significance. But before we look at the actual procedures, we need to study the history of pottery making. This week we benefit from the expert knowledge of Cynthia Bonner, talented potter and owner of Mud Hut Pottery:

> Ancient civilizations used earthenware clay to develop functional pots and platters. Traditional earthenware clay pieces were usually red—a blend of iron-rich clay compositions. Vitreous clay, such as porcelain and stoneware, was also discovered as a valuable clay medium. Pot shards revealing the story of ancient potters can be discovered across all parts of the world. Imagine digging up a centuries-old reddish-brown clay bowl without any glaze glossing over the fingerprints of the ancient potter who created it. The impression of the potter's hand remains on the bowl after thousands of years.

It is important to realize that clay is one of the most pliable and oldest art materials in the world. Clay is a natural decomposition of rock and one of the most abundant, inexpensive resources known to man. The creative possibilities for a lump of clay are almost endless to a skilled potter. Note that the potter has the freedom to form the clay however he or she desires. He or she has complete control over the creation of the pot, just as God has total control over the uniqueness of each individual before conception.

Romans 9:21 says, "Does not the potter have power over the clay, from the same lump to make one vessel for honor and another for dishonor?" In Greek, the word for "power over" is *exasla*, which means, "The right to act, decide, or dispose of one's property as one wishes."[2] This is a technical term used in establishing someone's will and testament. The Greek word for "the same lump" is *furamatos*, which means "that which is mixed or kneaded."[3] The potter has the right and ability to decide the outcome of whatever is mixed or kneaded. It is safe to say that the difference is not found in the clay itself, but in the potter's purpose.

If possible, find a piece of pottery this week, either in your own home or somewhere else. Take time to examine the details, character qualities, and purpose of the vessel. Do you think the product fulfilled the potter's design? For example, the pot may have been formed from a mixture of various red clays. You could describe it as a red vessel, but is it also red for another reason? Maybe red represented pain or agony to the potter. Perhaps you purchased a pot from an antique store because it went with the décor in your living room. Allow yourself

CREATED FOR GOD, BY GOD:
LIKE CLAY IN THE HANDS OF THE POTTER

to think back to the time it was created. Maybe a Native American created the pot as the family's sole cooking utensil. Can you visualize a woman using it to prepare meals throughout the winter? Ask the Lord to help you see past the obvious so you can realize a deeper spiritual truth hidden within the earthenware. Have fun this week as you experience "Created for God, by God"!

WEEK 2: DAY 1

THE TOUCH OF THE POTTER

You turn things upside down, as if the potter were thought to be like the clay! Shall what is formed say to Him who formed it, "He did not make me"? Can the pot say of the potter, "He knows nothing"?
—Isaiah 29:16

The first morning of our Alaskan cruise I secured a quiet location where I could view the scenery as I began composing the pages of this study. What a breathtaking place to write about God as the Creator of all things! I found myself captivated by the snow-covered mountains submerging themselves right into the ocean, spellbound by the whale breaking the surface to shoot water from his blowhole, and awestruck by a bald eagle gracefully soaring above. To top it off, the water's stillness resembled a sheet of ice.

As I continued writing, I began praising God out loud. I know the people around me probably thought I was delirious from seasickness and needed major counseling! The blessing of researching pottery and comparing the potter to God as the Creator put a song of praise in my soul.

As the morning waned, I noticed a crowd of people collecting in one area of the deck. Curious, I made my way in their direction. As I moved closer, my mouth nearly dropped to the ground. My eyes focused on a man sitting at a potter's wheel, with his gentle hands forming a vessel from a wet lump of clay. Immediately, shock passed through my body. He could have been demonstrating anything—glass blowing, jewelry making, painting. But God, in His infinite way of working things to His glory, orchestrated a divine appointment for me.

There on a cruise ship off the coast of Alaska, God provided a potter at his spinning wheel to give me a "hands-on" lesson the very day I started writing "Touch of the Potter." Oh, we serve an amazing Savior, Jesus, who is alive and active in our lives! Look for Him in the midst of your day. Keep your eyes open to the tender moments the Lord has in store for you!

As you work through the steps of creating a unique piece of pottery, it is vital to keep in mind that without the potter, the lump of clay remains just that—a lump. Today we will focus all of our attention on the analogy of the potter to God as the Creator. I encourage you to first spend some moments in prayer, seeking the Lord's guidance with a humbleness to hear from the Holy Spirit.

Scripture Excavation

Read Genesis 1:26–2:7. Paraphrase this block of Scripture in your own words and add any thoughts that come to mind regarding God as the Creator of Man.

_____

_____

As we dig deeper into Genesis 2:7, we discover some very valuable treasures. The Hebrew word for "formed" is *yatsar*, which means to form, fashion, or frame. The word for "dust" is `*aphar*, which means dry or loose earth, powder, ashes, ground mortar, or rubbish. God as the Creator chose to fashion His design, this human being, out of dry and loose earth and to breathe life into him. This is almost identical to how a potter forms a piece of earthenware and artistically fashions his or her vessel. He or she takes clay from the ground, works with it until it is the proper consistency, and places it in the center of his or her potter's wheel. As the wheel begins to turn, the firm but gentle pressure from the potter's hands molds the vessel into shape. Water is periodically thrown onto the earthenware so that it will maintain the appropriate consistency—too dry makes it rigid and too wet makes it lifeless. It is worth noting that in both instances of creation, the raw material comes from the same source: the earth. Thank God for what He is teaching you this week!

Now that we have a clearer understanding of the words "formed" and "dust," let's excavate an intriguing block of Scripture. Read Jeremiah 1:4–10. Rewrite Jeremiah 1:5, inserting one of the explanations above for the word "formed" and write your thoughts.

_____

_____

Notice in verse 6 that the Lord doesn't reprimand Jeremiah when he says, "I cannot speak, I am only a youth." God simply confirms to him in verse 7 that He is in control of where He sends Jeremiah and He will give him the words to speak. How sweet! If you were Jeremiah and God spoke verse 8 to you, how would you respond?

_____

_____

Consider what it must have been like for Jeremiah to have the Lord tenderly touch his lips. Was the touch powerful, sensitive, firm, warm, or compassionate? Let your heart connect with God as you write your thoughts.

_____

_____

Have you ever experienced God's touch on your lips? Is there a time you can remember, an encounter with almighty God, when He spoke through your vocal cords so that His purposes could be accomplished? Have fun journaling about God's touch on your life!

_____

_____

Hidden Treasures

Read 2 Corinthians 4:7 and take time to meditate on what the Lord has shown you today about God forming man from the earth, then compare it with a potter fashioning his vessel from the same substance. Write your thoughts, asking God to breathe life into them as you focus on God as the Creator.

_____

_____

Do you have a difficult time viewing yourself as "God's tender creation" and masterpiece? Write your thoughts on how the Lord views you as His creation.

_____

_____

What do you think you would be like if God had not sculpted you?

_____

_____

Celebrating Treasured Gifts

Ask the Holy Spirit to enlighten you and illuminate the truth of the Scriptures. You want to see personal applications of God's Word in your daily walk with Him. In other words, strive to understand what the Lord is teaching you and how you can incorporate His truths into your thoughts and actions. With heartfelt tenderness, write a prayer to God, expressing the things you sense Him teaching you today. Take time to praise God as the Creator of all. He loves for us to express to Him the intimacy of our love, appreciation, and praises.

_____

_____

_____

_____

_____

Reflection Pause

The potter begins the process of creating his handiwork with a purpose for each new mass of clay. He starts with a determination to properly prepare his equipment, hand tools, potter's wheel, clay, water, glazes, kiln, etc. It is vital that you realize the importance of the manner in which the potter works with the clay. If the potter is too rough, the clay will become rigid and stiff. On the other hand, if he does not press on the clay enough to remove the impurities, it has the potential to become too soft and unresponsive to his molding.

God, the Master Potter, molds His children in a similar manner. Jeremiah's life is an example of how God had a plan to create and mold a man to use him as a prophet to the nations. When Jeremiah was a young boy, he had no idea that God was developing within him the qualities he needed to become a mighty messenger to the people of Israel. Be encouraged, sister-friend: God had a plan before you came into existence! Seek Him daily. He is waiting to share His plan with you. Today, experience the Master Potter's touch in your life and see Him working in your everyday activities.

WEEK 2: DAY 2

THE LUMP OF CLAY

We are the clay, you are the potter; we are all the work of your hand.

—Isaiah 64:8

Is your life going in every direction? Is your agenda set days in advance? Do you wonder if it ever will slow down so that you can catch your breath? We live in a fast-paced world where everything seems to happen at the touch of a button. It's almost as if we snap our fingers and things move into action—the snooze alarm wakes us, the preset coffee maker perks, the microwave heats breakfast, the automatic opener lifts the garage door, the MP3 player loaded with thousands of songs entertains us while we drive, and the list goes on and on. (Some of you might remember eight-track tape players—with those, you waited at least four songs to hear your favorite!) We are a fast-paced society that expects things to happen immediately. We have lost, in many ways, the ability to learn and practice patience.

What are we teaching our children? What is modeled before their very eyes? How can God mold us into His vessels when we are moving in so many directions?

Yesterday we had the opportunity to focus on the potter. Remember, without the potter, the clay would still be in its original state. Today we shift our focus to the clay.

Cynthia Bonner explains how the potter prepares the clay:

> The potter has to decide what to do with the clay to achieve the final product he has in mind. First, the texture of the clay mixture must be consistent and free of air pockets. If it is too wet, the clay won't hold a shape; if too dry, it cracks and can't be shaped. Mixing the clay and temper to form the prepared or ready-to-use clay is similar to kneading dough when you are making bread. Once mixed together, the clay will actually improve as it ages, but it can also be used right away. In the pottery process, the potter can choose either the "hand-built" method or the "thrown on the wheel" technique. With "hand-building," one has the opportunity to realize the full potential of every aspect of sculpting the structure. This is usually a more time-consuming process but yields beautiful results. The "throwing method" begins with successfully throwing properly prepared clay. The first step in producing properly prepared clay is "wedging" or "kneading" the balls of clay. Poorly wedged clay does not respond well to the molding process. By applying pressure on the clay, the potter eliminates air bubbles that can cause problems down the road.

Before we look at today's scripture, ask God to open your heart to His teaching, and surrender your will to His will. Let Jesus mold you as you move through this study. Praise Him for what He plans to teach you!

Scripture Excavation

Let's look again at Jeremiah 1:4–10 and also at verses 11–19. What was Jeremiah like before God revealed His plans for him? Don't forget the analogy of believers to the potter's clay.

_____

_____

Focus in on verses 11–13. This is an example of the heart of this Bible study. God used familiar visuals to help Jeremiah grasp His teaching. What were these visuals, and why were they important?

_____

_____

Jeremiah 2–14 focuses on Jeremiah pleading with the Israelites to repent and return to the Mosaic Covenant. God spoke through Jeremiah as he urged the Jews to turn from their sins of idol worship, selfishness, and pride, and warned them of God's judgment. How frustrating for Jeremiah that he didn't see positive results! Read Jeremiah 15:10–21 and share your thoughts.

_____

_____

You might be thinking, *Sure God could use Jeremiah, because He called Jeremiah into His service as a young man. Jeremiah didn't have a sinful past like mine.* Let's turn to the New Testament and look at the life of a man with a very sinful past, one whom God used for the kingdom in a mighty way. Look at Acts 9:1–22. What was Paul like before meeting Jesus on the Damascus Road? What was he like after his encounter with Jesus?

_____

_____

Examine Acts 9:15 again. Think about the relationship between the potter and his clay, and comment on this verse. Look back at Jeremiah 1:5.

_____

_____

Paul allowed Jesus to mold him into a powerful voice for the kingdom, even though he had been a vigorous persecutor of Jesus' followers before his conversion. I love the fact that Paul didn't use his past as an excuse to ignore God's plan for him to proclaim Jesus as the Savior of the world. Many times God uses our past to fashion us into mighty vessels for His glory. Amen!

From a human point of view, it might appear that Jeremiah failed in his efforts to bring the Israelites to repentance for their rebellion against God. They continued to reject God's words as spoken by Jeremiah, and they maintained their sinful ways. But from a spiritual standpoint, Jeremiah became a proven and faithful servant whose trust in God never wavered, even when he didn't see results. God called him to be a prophet and to serve as His voice to the nation of Israel. Throughout Jeremiah's ministry to the Israelites, God continued to mold his willing heart. Jeremiah experienced rejection, abuse, imprisonment, threats, and more, all because he was doing exactly what God called him to do. Moreover, he didn't allow circumstances to affect his overwhelming trust in God.

I love that Jeremiah didn't throw in the towel when he experienced discouragement in his ministry. At times he became weary because he didn't see a change in the people. But through God's gentleness, Jeremiah received the encouragement he needed to follow God's direction for his life. Jeremiah 15 begins with God spurring on a downcast Jeremiah towards the work He wanted him to accomplish. God encouraged Jeremiah. Then in verse 16, Jeremiah responded: "Your words were found, and I ate them, and Your word was to me the joy and rejoicing of my heart; For I am called by Your name." How precious! God encourages us with His Word when we need it the most!

Hidden Treasures

As you answered the questions in Day 2's Scripture Excavation section, I hope you noticed the important messages in the passages. What did God teach you today? On a daily basis, does God or the world in which you live more easily mold you? Take time to consider these questions and answer honestly.

_____

_____

_____

_____

Celebrating Treasured Gifts

Just as the potter kneads his clay to remove air bubbles, so God wedges us. Can you feel Him pressing in on you to remove the areas that could make you a weak vessel rather than a strong basin? What are some of these "air bubbles" that need to be wedged out of your life?

Thank You, heavenly God, for how You are molding me through . . .

_____

_____

_____

_____

_____

Reflection Pause

God's gentle way of dealing with Jeremiah is similar to the way the potter works with his or her clay. The potter has to knead or wedge the clay gently to remove all of the air bubbles so that the vessel will be solid and without flaws. Any potter knows that the air bubbles or pockets of emptiness left in a pot will cause it to be brittle and easily broken when it is placed in the kiln. God wanted Jeremiah to stay focused on Him rather than the people.

God works in the same way today. Are you feeling frustration because, although you are serving the Lord, you aren't seeing any visible results? Maybe you're a young mom, and day after day you discipline your child without seeing any changes in his or her behavior. You may become discouraged and think you might as well give up. Stop right there! Run to God, and ask Him to be your encourager. Look for ways He spurs you forward in motherhood. Let Him guide every step of your life. God designed your life before conception. Believe it!

WEEK 2: DAY 3

THE SPINNING OF THE WHEEL

We are the clay, you are the potter; we are all the work of your hand.

—Isaiah 64:8

As the mother of three sons, I have plenty of experience in raising boys. One day I had the opportunity to share this knowledge with a mom's group. Prior to this event, I'd been dealing with the embarrassing issue of uncontrollable perspiration during my speaking engagements. I heard about a well-known speaker who used mini pads in the armpits of her shirt or jacket to protect her from this condition. With excitement, I knew I had found my answer! As I shared this remedy with my mom, I heard a hesitation in her voice. In her gentle way, she warned me that this solution might have its own problems.

"Armed" and ready to go, I proceeded forward with these moms. At the conclusion of the day, the ladies started exiting the room as I quickly put my belongings away. All of a sudden, I swung my arm around, and to my surprise, out flew one of the mini pads. It landed on the floor right in front of the first row of chairs. Words cannot describe the horror I felt at that moment! As I picked up the evidence, the thought occurred to me, *Where is the other one?* I promptly thrust my hand down into my jacket sleeve, but I couldn't locate the second pad. In my mind, I caught a glimpse of it plummeting from my sleeve right in the midst of my sharing my passion for mothering. At that point I noticed something peeking out from the end of my sleeve. I grabbed it and stuffed both of them into my purse, all the time thanking the Lord that no one had observed this mishap.

On the drive home, the thought came to me that this is an example of trying to hide something ungodly in my heart. If not dealt with, ideas I thought were hidden might come spewing from my mouth to the dismay of everyone nearby. Wow! God uses *all* things to teach us important life lessons, but we must be willing to see beyond the obvious circumstances. Perhaps the most important lesson for me: I am never too old to heed my mother's wise words of advice. Amen!

This week we examined the potter's purpose for his or her clay and the importance of the clay staying moldable throughout the shaping process. Today we turn our attention to the potter's wheel. Sometimes during the pottery process, the wheel must be immobile to create exceptional character. Yet at other times, the apparatus must rotate quickly to mold with precision. The potter decides what to do, depending on each pot's purpose.

Today, the wheel represents different circumstances in our lives. Sometimes life seems to be at a standstill, and other times it is spinning out of control. Ask the Lord for an open mind and heart today as you learn about "The Spinning of the Wheel."

Cynthia Bonner explains:

> The potter's wheel is an apparatus with a large, flat, circular top that rotates in a particular direction at varied speeds. Centering the clay on the wheel is a critical step in the process. The purpose of the centering procedure is to shape and compress the clay into a symmetrical mass perfectly centered in the middle of the wheel. This involves the potter's full concentration and requires the weight of the potter's arm muscles. At this point, if not properly centered, the lump of clay can go flying into orbit as the wheel launches into action. To an inexperienced thrower, this could be a surprise! After properly centering the lump of clay, the potter is ready to form an original vessel. The mass of clay is penetrated to create a V-shaped opening, and then the piece is formed by lifting the pot's walls. The potter must maintain a firm and steady upward movement by locking his hands together. This allows him to form a lifting tool with his hands as he moves and thins the clay. On the potter's wheel, he can produce large numbers of handmade functional wares. Even though the wheel aids in establishing symmetry and precision, every piece produced is unique and never exactly the same as the previous ones. All pottery creations are indeed individual creations.

Scripture Excavation

Turn once again to the New Testament. Read Matthew 8:23–27, Mark 4:35–41, and Luke 8:22–25.

In your own words, describe the scene. What different personalities were in the boat? What were the weather conditions and physical conditions? What else is pertinent?

_____

_____

The Sea of Galilee is a wide lake that is situated way below sea level. The mountains framing the lake create a vortex or wind tunnel into the lake. From a bird's eye view, it looks like a body of water that is simple to cross. But the winds can produce nighttime storms caused by warm air rising from the lake and colliding with cooler mountain air. This collision often creates unexpected storms with turbulent winds and high waves. The disciples knew these facts, yet they showed faith in Jesus by getting into the boat to go with Him to the other side of the lake, even though it was close to dusk.

With that information in mind, pick one of the disciples and write a short summary of what he might have been thinking as he climbed into the boat. Have fun with this question and remember the disciples' different personalities.

_____

_____

It is important to read all of the gospel passages (Matthew, Mark, Luke, and John) that mention the same event because you get different viewpoints and occasionally additional information. For example, Jesus' calming the storm is recorded in Matthew 8:23–27, Mark 4:35–41, and Luke 8:22–25. It is written by three different men with three different perspectives. What are some of the facts mentioned in one passage but not in another?

_____

_____

Where in the boat was Jesus located when the storm appeared? Why is this significant?

_____

_____

As the storm started building, imagine the thoughts going through the disciples' minds, such as fearing for their lives, lack of trust, and doubts that Jesus could save them. Notice that in Mark 4:37 and 39 in the NKJV, the word "great" is used in both verses. It describes a "great storm" and a "great calm." The Greek word for "great" is *megas,* which means "splendid, prepared on a grand scale, stately."[4] What would it have been like to experience both of these extremes in such a short period of time?

_____

_____

Hidden Treasures

Look back at the block of scriptures we studied in the Scripture Excavation section. Compare the use of the potter's wheel with the situation the disciples were in when they obeyed Jesus and traveled across the lake with Him. Be prepared—God has something very special to teach you through this lesson. Allow your heart to open to His edification!

I hope you realize that Jesus is "in the boat" with you in every situation. It is up to you to ask Him to lead you through your life's voyage. He will not push Himself on anyone, but He waits for you to call out His name. What did Jesus allow the disciples to experience while He slept? What happened after the disciples woke Jesus?

_____

_____

REFLECTING HIM

Think of a boat in which God has placed you. Which individuals are in the boat with you? Maybe it's your family, friends, a church committee, Bible study group, mission trip group, prayer group, etc.

_____
_____
_____

What are the different personalities? Are there different perspectives?

_____
_____
_____

Just as Jesus allowed this stormy situation we see in Scripture, He has a purpose for your tempestuous moments. Permit the pressures of the turbulent experiences in your "boat" to knit your group together rather than pull it apart. The ways of the world and Satan are to sever relationships; in contrast, God's will is to unify believers. Jesus gave His disciples the opportunity to put into action what He had taught them through the parables. He does the same with us today. Once we learn something from our Christian walk, God will give us opportunities to move into a deeper relationship with Him. These real-life experiences sometimes have us spinning like the potter's wheel. Get excited—God is forming you into His masterpiece to be used for His purposes!

Celebrating Treasured Gifts

In the Hidden Treasures section of Day 1, you read 2 Corinthians 4:7, which confirmed that Christians are fragile pottery—not expensive, but weak and breakable. This type of pottery refers to dust and particles of the earth. Jesus' light shines through us—cracked pieces of pottery—while we live in this world. This is not by our power but by God's. Now read 2 Corinthians 4:7–18. Considering today's Hidden Treasure, journal what God is saying to you through these verses. (Note: The Greek word for "hard pressed" is *thlibo*, which means afflicted, pressed in, compression. Do any of these words sound familiar?)

_____
_____
_____
_____
_____

Reflection Pause

Think back to our analogy with the potter's wheel. It is when the wheel is rotating that the potter actually forms the clay into a beautiful creation. If the clay could talk, it might say that it didn't like the spinning part because of how fast it turned and the uncomfortable pressure from the potter's hands. But if this process didn't happen, the clay would remain an unformed lump, and the potter's purpose for the clay never would be fulfilled.

Earlier, Cynthia Bonner said, "The potter must maintain a firm and steady upwards movement by locking his hands together to form a *lifting tool* with his hands as he moves and thins the clay" (emphasis mine). Just as the potter's hands lift the original lump of clay while it spins on the center of the wheel, God places His hand on you to lift you from hopeless situations and experiences in your life. The key is to choose to remain in the center of His will—or I should say His "wheel"?

Wow! Thank God for His gentle lifting hand that is on your life.

WEEK 2: DAY 4

THE UNIQUENESS OF IMPERFECTIONS

We are the clay, you are the potter; we are all the work of your hand.

—Isaiah 64:8

Each piece of pottery is unique and full of imperfections. On Day 1 you were to find a piece of pottery to examine. If you have it close by, take time to analyze it one more time. Notice the vessel's distinguishing features—the hues and rare designs that make the piece one of a kind. The end of Cynthia Bonner's quote on Day 3 said, "Every piece produced is unique and never exactly the same as the previous ones. All pottery creations are indeed individual creations."

She goes on to share how pressure affects the pot:

> The potter shapes the vessel by applying pressure inside and/or outside the walls as he lifts. Remember that with every pressure action there is a reaction in the clay. The walls can move in or out depending on the pressure made by the potter's motions. He may throw a bowl, plate, vase, bottle, or pitcher; he may form a pedestal at the foot of a pot, a belly in the center, or a neck at the rim. The pot's shape depends on the clay's capabilities and the potter's skills. When the pot is a "leather-hard" consistency, the potter can trim and decorate the ware. With an eye to detail, the potter trims and designs a finished piece that enhances the pot's individual beauty. The creative possibilities are limitless—an expression of the potter's imagination. Each ceramic piece goes through multiple stages of development and decoration. The glazing process is especially critical. A glazed surface provides the final finished look to the product. When you glaze a piece of pottery, there are endless possibilities to consider, such as color, shine intensity, and surface saturation. Glazes are glass with various modifiers added to affect their appearance—gloss, semi-gloss, mat, or semi-mat. These add texture and uniqueness to the appearance. Glaze color alone involves multiple ranges of hue and intensity or brightness. The choice of the glaze and the manner by which it is applied (dipping glazes, brushing glazes, pouring glazes) ultimately will determine the ceramic pot's final appearance. The opportunities for experimenting with color and surface texture are endless.

Scripture Excavation

Keep the description of adding pressure to the clay in the forefront of your mind as you read Isaiah 64:8 with Romans 9:20–21. Compare these two scriptures with the final steps in the pottery process. Be creative, and ask God to emboss His fingerprint on your heart as you write. This is so much fun—just like a treasure hunt! There is excitement with each new piece of evidence we uncover.

_____

_____

Now read Isaiah 29:15–16 and 45:9–10. What is similar in both of these verses, and what is the tone in which they were written? (Note: The word "potsherd" in the Hebrew is *cheres* and means clay pottery, earthenware, shard, earthen vessel.)

_____

_____

Travel to the New Testament, and let's look at a very familiar person in Scripture, John the Baptist. Read Mark 1:1–11 and Luke 1:5–25; 39–45; 57–80. Did God have a purpose in mind when he created John the Baptist? Referring to these specific verses, explain your thoughts.

_____

_____

THE UNIQUENESS OF IMPERFECTIONS

What is significant about Luke 1:31–45?

_____
_____

When God has a plan He is accomplishing through His children, no one can stop God's will from being fulfilled; not even a doubtful father like Zechariah in Luke 1:18–20. Amen!

What unique qualities did John the Baptist possess that made him stand out in the crowd?

_____
_____

Hidden Treasures

Compare Cynthia Bonner's description of the importance of pressure to John the Baptist's life. What are the similarities of this phase of pottery creation to John's life? This might seems like a difficult question, so ask the Holy Spirit to help you see beyond the words to the heart of what God wants to teach you.

_____
_____

Do you have some unique character qualities? Describe ways in which God might use them or ways He has used them in the past.

_____
_____

In Mark 1:4 and Luke 1:80, the word "desert" comes from the Greek root word *eremos,* which means solitary, lonely, desolate, or uninhabited. Read both verses again and insert one of these adjectives in front of the word "desert." What Hidden Treasures do you find?

_____
_____

Celebrating Treasured Gifts

I am trying very hard to hold back from blurting out what the Lord taught me through this passage. OK, I can't stand it! I have to share one of God's messages with you. It is amazing to me that God allowed John to grow up in the desert—a lonely, solitary, desolate place. But this allowed him to understand and experience physical loneliness as well as spiritual isolation. John knew God personally and understood God's purpose for his life. Because of John's experiences in the desert, he was able to recognize the loneliness and spiritual anguish of the people coming from Judea and Jerusalem to be baptized by him.

REFLECTING HIM

Before John the Baptist's birth, God prepared him to be a mighty voice to proclaim the Messiah's coming. God trained John his entire life. His parents, the environment in which he grew up, his "out of the norm" personality, and every part of his existence led up to the purpose God intended for John the Baptist.

Do you have a hard time accepting that you are unique, one of a kind, and born into your family for a specific reason? God's design has given you special physical features too, and just like John, God has a purpose for your life, designed by Him for Him. Why do we strive for perfection when God is all the while calling imperfect people to be His vessels? Do you find yourself looking horizontally at others and coveting their exceptional qualities? Instead, focus upward to the Lord in gratitude for the gifts (and imperfections) He has given you. Take some time to think about these questions and all that you have studied today, and write a summary of your thoughts. Don't forget to add insights gained from what you've learned about pottery this week.

_____

_____

_____

_____

_____

_____

Reflection Pause

Did John experience frustration because of his one-of-a-kind character, his distinctive temperament, and his rare disposition? Did he stop sharing the message about the Messiah because he thought others might think he was crazy or mad? No, the fact is that John the Baptist didn't focus on himself. He concentrated on his calling from God to prepare the way for the Messiah's coming. I love how God works! John and Jesus were cousins of almost the same age—I'm sure they spent time together playing children's games, laughing, eating at the same table, etc. Think about what it is like at your family events and how the children enjoy spending time together. Imagine being at a family reunion with Jesus! I bet John never worried that Jesus might take away his toys. For thirty years they spent special moments together, but more than likely John had no idea Jesus was the Messiah. Can you envision the look on John's face when Jesus walked up to him to be baptized, and the Holy Spirit revealed, "This is the one you have been waiting for, John!"

Are you beginning to grasp that you were "Created for God, by God"? Today, celebrate the treasured gifts from God that are unique to you alone. You are one of a kind and designed exactly in God's image.

WEEK 2: DAY 5

THE FIRING PROCESS

We are the clay, you are the potter; we are all the work of your hand.

—Isaiah 64:8

When my precious daughter first started cooking, she decided to bake a cake for her daddy all by herself. What a sweet idea! She wanted him to be proud of her. Excitedly, she measured and mixed the ingredients. Then she poured the mixture into the pan and put it in the oven. With great anticipation, she waited for her masterpiece to bake. When the timer buzzed, she proudly opened the door to the oven. Immediately, a look of disappointment washed over her face. The cake looked exactly as it did when she put it in the oven. Bless her heart! She had left out a crucial part of the baking process: turning on the oven.

My daughter learned a valuable lesson that day—without heat, the batter will stay in its original state. However, with the right temperature, the mixture will transform into a scrumptious cake, tantalizing people with its smell, sight, and taste.

It is the same with pottery making. The firing process is essential for the earthenware to reach its full potential. After the piece is removed from the oven, its colors, hues, shape, and purpose are revealed. Isn't this what happens in our Christian lives? We must go through some fiery trials so others will see a beautifully finished product with a tag that reads, "Specially made by the hands of Jesus."

Our study on pottery making is not complete without an examination of "The Firing Process." Today we focus on the final step in creating a piece of earthenware and compare that course of action to the sanctification process in the Christian life.

Before we continue, it is vital that you fully understand this fact: The moment you accept Jesus as Lord and Savior of your life, you are His forever. Your eternal position in heaven is secure because of His work on the cross and your faith in Jesus Christ, God's Son. By trusting Jesus as your Savior, you now have a personal relationship with God forever. Nothing you can do will remove your eternal position:

> For I am persuaded that neither death nor life, nor angels nor principalities nor powers, nor things present nor things to come, nor height nor depth, nor any other created thing, shall be able to separate us from the love of God which is in Christ Jesus our Lord.
>
> —Romans 8:38–39 NKJV

The sanctification process is the condition of your relationship with Jesus. Think about your relationship with your mother. From the moment of conception you were connected to her. She gave birth to you, or perhaps you were lovingly adopted. Nothing can take that away from you—it is your position with your mother. The relationship is dependent on interaction with one another. Time spent together deepens that connection. But if something happens after a while that harms or hurts the relationship, the fact remains that she is still your mother.

Your relationship with Jesus works the same way. The more time you spend in His Word, prayer, praise, worship, and fellowship with other believers, the more immersed your walk with Christ becomes. As a result, the relationship's condition strengthens on a daily basis. See where I am going? This is such an important concept to grasp! It frees you from the bondage of thinking that your position depends on your performance as a Christian. Praise God, it is all about Him and not about us!

Cynthia Bonner explains how a pot is fired:

> Once glazed, a pot is fired in the kiln. This is a time of thrill and discovery. With proper knowledge and training, a potter can manage the firing process with great success. However, all firings are unpredictable to some extent—so all potters learn to accept and find joy in this unpredictable element in the process of creating a piece of pottery. It is at this point where the prepared, wedged clay is tested; if the wedging process has not removed air bubbles from the clay, then the clay might not withstand the high firing temperature and could fall apart. As a result, opening a kiln with fired wares is similar to Christmas Day—there is always a beautiful surprise that never can be recreated. It is a totally unique gift to be celebrated and enjoyed!

With the final stages of pottery in the forefront of your mind and the discussion of the sanctification process fresh, ask the Lord to ready your heart to receive new insights as you study more about "The Firing Process."

THE FIRING PROCESS

Scripture Excavation

Throughout the Bible there are many references to fire, which means a burning product that produces heat, light, and flame. God often used fire in His metaphors. For example, Hebrews 12:29 says, "For our 'God is a consuming fire,'" referring to the Lord and His discipline of His people. Then in Acts 2:3 it says, "They saw what seemed to be tongues of fire that separated and came to rest on each of them."

The people of the Bible understood fire's significance to their God. On the Mount of Olives, God consumed Elijah's offering with fire to show His power over Baal and other false gods (see 1 Kings 18:38–39). God used a pillar of fire to guide the children of Israel at night (see Ex. 13:21–22). And, of course, we can't leave out the famous burning bush that appeared to Moses (see Ex. 3). In the English language, "purify" is similar to the New Testament Greek word often used for fire, giving still another definition. God used fire to show His power and strength, His relationship with His people, and His judgment and purification. Our God is so creative!

Let's narrow our focus to a well-known Scripture passage regarding fire: the story of the fiery furnace.

To begin, read Daniel 3:8–30. In your own words, write a short summary of these verses. Include background information, the main characters, the supporting characters, their attitudes, etc.

_____

_____

_____

_____

_____

_____

How does God use fire in this situation?

_____

_____

Focus on Daniel 3:19. Before Shadrach, Meshach, and Abednego were thrown into the furnace, what were Nebuchadnezzar's orders?

_____

_____

What happened to the guards when they opened the furnace doors?

_____

_____

Think for a moment: Which group was successful in the heat of the situation—the worshipers of the one true God or the non-believers? Define a spiritual concept God is teaching through this event. Go to town with this question, and let the Lord show you something very special!

_____

_____

Who was in the fire with the friends, and who watched from a distance?

_____

_____

Hidden Treasures

Get ready for some amazing realizations to unfold in your heart as we dig deeper into the meaning of Daniel 3:8–25. Let's compare the sanctification process in the Christian life to the firing process of pottery.

Throughout Shadrach, Meshach, and Abednego's captivity in Babylon, God continued to mold them into vessels He could use for His purposes. Finally, they had to make a choice: serve the one true God or bow to the king's gods. These three men displayed a strong faith and total trust in God to deliver them from the fire. God's testing of their faith led to purification through the fiery experience. As a result, the king decreed that no one could speak against the God of Shadrach, Meshach, and Abednego. (This is a short summary of an event packed with many lessons!)

Does something pop out of this passage that you can apply to your life? What "fiery situation" does the world use to tempt you? What lessons can you learn from this scripture to help you to handle them?

_____

_____

Are you in a situation now, or have you ever been, in which you made a choice to follow God? As a result, did the fire get seven times hotter? Explain your answer.

_____

_____

These friends had each other in the furnace. Whom has God allowed to walk with you in your fiery trial?

_____

_____

It is such a blessing when we share our experiences with one another. God uses them to comfort others, bring glory to Himself, deepen relationships, and help people get real!

Celebrating Treasured Gifts

What practical lesson will you be able to use as you abide in Christ on a daily basis?

_____

_____

THE FIRING PROCESS

Which day of "Created for God, by God" was most meaningful to you: The Touch of the Potter, The Lump of Clay, The Spinning of the Wheel, The Uniqueness of Imperfections, or The Firing Process? Explain.

_____

_____

Write a personal prayer to the Lord, thanking Him for what He has taught you about Himself, as well as thanking Him for the purpose He has for your life.

_____

_____

_____

_____

_____

_____

_____

Reflection Pause

Do you see Jesus walking with you in the heat of your situation? He is there, I promise! Notice that the three friends didn't see Jesus while they were in the fiery furnace, but others did see Him walking with them. God sometimes allows others to see inside your situation so that their faith will grow, and He will receive the glory!

I love that Shadrach, Meshach, and Abednego walked around in the fire. They didn't sit or stand, but they kept moving as their hands were freed from their bindings. With excitement, I can say that they came out of the fire unharmed! Their clothes were not singed, nor did they smell of smoke. God received all the glory from their experience!

It's the same with a fired piece of earthenware—the heat completes the process. Think about this: When a clay pot is removed from the kiln, the smell of smoke is not on it. Only the physical change to the surface of the pot is visible. Praise God for the fiery situations in your life, that others might see the beauty God is creating in you. Amen!

WEEK 3

SENSES OF THE SOUL: THE TOUCH, AROMA, TASTE, SIGHT, AND SOUND OF JESUS

You shall love the Lord your God with all your heart, with all your soul, and with all your mind.
—Matthew 22:37 NKJV

Jesus satisfies the senses of touch, aroma, taste, sight, and sound of the soul. How would you describe the human soul? For centuries, this topic has been explored from every religious perspective, psychological point of view, and medical angle. Some ancient Greeks viewed the human soul as a person's core, the place where behavior is determined. Throughout history there have been many other beliefs about the human soul, but our objective this week is to focus only on God's definition.

The verse above, Matthew 22:37, is a wonderful place to begin our journey. This verse gives hints to discovering God's purpose for equipping the physical body with an inner soul. In this passage, a group of Pharisees confronts Jesus. A lawyer asks Jesus a question: "Which is the greatest commandment in the law?" Eloquently, Jesus answers to love God with your whole being—your heart, soul, and mind.

It is imperative when studying Scripture to understand the original meaning of the words. We accomplish this by exploring the Hebrew definitions when studying the Old Testament and the Greek definitions for the New Testament. *Strong's Exhaustive Concordance of the Bible*[5] gives these Greek definitions for Matthew 22:37:

- Heart—*Kardia*. The vigor and sense of physical life; your will.
- Soul—*Psuche*. The seat of feelings, desires, affections, aversions; the breath of life.
- Mind—*Dianoia*. The faculty of understanding, feeling, desiring; intellectual.

These definitions give us greater insight into the meanings behind each word, allowing the truth to shine through. So this verse in Matthew could be translated to say, "You shall love the Lord your God with all your will, with all your affection, and with all your understanding."

This week's study focuses on the soul. The Old Testament provides an even deeper appreciation for the meaning of the word. Read Deuteronomy 6:5. In the Hebrew, we find *soul/nephesh* means self, life, person, mind, desire, living being; that which breathes; seat of the appetites, emotions, and passions.

Hold on to your chair as you read Genesis 2:7 (NKJV): "And the Lord God formed man of the dust of the ground, and breathed into his nostrils the *breath of life*; and man became a living being" (emphasis mine). Do you see that *breath of life* could be a substitute for the word *soul*? God breathed into His human creation the soul—the seat of appetites, emotions, and passions. I love it! God is the giver, and we are the recipients. God gives us our soul before conception. He sent Jesus into the world as the only one qualified to fill the soul through a personal relationship. Amen!

Vivid life descriptions help us to grasp a deeper knowledge of God's precepts. For example, the *soul* each person is born with can be compared to a deflated balloon. All our lives we strive to discover what it takes to blow up that empty *soul* balloon. Many believe that money, success, knowledge, materialism, relationships, or family are the keys to a fulfilled life. But these criteria fall short of filling the void. It is only when we surrender our lives to Jesus as our Lord and Savior that He breathes the breath of life into our vacant *soul* balloon. It immediately becomes filled to capacity with Jesus and the Holy Spirit. We are now equipped with the Holy Spirit's omnipresent gifts, and we are stamped with a seal that emphatically states, "Marked with the blood of Jesus! Now Jesus' Forever!" (Read Ephesians 4:30.) As a believer, relish the fact that your soul has become 100 percent complete. It is awe-inspiring to realize that as you seek to deepen your relationship with the Lord, the balloon becomes filled to capacity with completeness and contentment. Amen!

The Human Sensory System

God created the human body with a variety of systems to control different areas. The human sensory system controls the main senses of the body: touch, sight, hearing, smell, and taste. These five basic senses connect our physical bodies to our environments.

We have some thrilling discoveries ahead this week as we view each area of the human sensory system. Get ready to learn some amazing facts about the eyes, the electrifying sense of touch, the truths about our taste buds, the audio phenomenon, and how the brain responds to thousands of odors. Ask the Lord to prepare your heart for what He has in store as you leap into "Senses of the Soul."

WEEK 3: DAY 1

OPEN THE EYES OF MY SOUL

The eye is the lamp of the body.

—Matthew 6:22

Recently, while speaking at a women's retreat, I met a beautiful sister in Christ who has been blind from birth. Sitting on the front row, she soaked in every word I said. Her precious sounds of affirmation totally touched my heart. Upon our introduction, she immediately began to feel the shape and contour of my hands and face. Then she said, "Oh, I see Jesus in you! Please understand I don't need physical eyes to see the anointing of the Lord. He has given me eyes to the soul."

I embraced her with tender gentleness as tears trickled down my face. Those who know me would find this hard to believe, but I found myself completely speechless. I thank God for the opportunity to meet a sister in Christ who doesn't have to physically see God's evidence but can spiritually see God through the eyes of her soul. Wow, may we all learn from this precious child of the King.

Take a moment to scan the area around you. What colors do you see as you slowly view one thing and then another? It's interesting how the various images and colors constantly shift as you turn your head. At first glance it appears that each image blends into the next. In reality, your eyes and brain are continually updating the image. The human sensory system of vision views images so rapidly that a break in the action can't even be recognized. The eye/brain connection has the ability to see a wide range of colors, observe the flow of picture-perfect motion, and understand minute-by-minute details, all within a split second. God blessed His creations with a unique way to view the world in which we live. Ask the Holy Spirit to open your soul's eyes so that you can see what God desires to teach you through His Word.

Real Life Facts[6]

- All parts of the body change as we grow, except for the eye.
- The human eye's size doesn't change from the time we are born.
- The average person blinks 10,080 times every fourteen hours.
- An eagle can see a rabbit about 1,760 yards away, but the average human can only see the rabbit from 550 yards away.
- The eye has more than two million working parts and processes 36,000 bits of information every hour.
- The most complex organ in the human body, aside from the brain, is the eye.
- In a sighted person, eighty-five percent of his or her total knowledge results from vision.
- The eyeball in a human adult measures one inch in diameter but only one-sixth of it is exposed.
- Our eyes use sixty-five percent of the total pathways to our brain!

Scripture Excavation

There are numerous references to the eye in both the Old and New Testaments. David said, "I will set before my eyes no vile thing" (Ps. 101:3). Ephesians says, "The eyes of your heart may be enlightened, in order that you may know the hope to which He has called you" (1:18). Today, as we tunnel through a variety of scriptures, be prepared to receive what the Lord has planned as you "Open the Eyes of Your Soul."

There is no better place to begin than at the beginning of the Bible. Read Genesis 3:1–7. List all references to the eye, eyes, and "saw." What is significant about each statement?

Saw the fruit (evil) Eyes were opened—by lack of faith & belief.
(soul)

What spiritual meaning does God give to the word "eyes" in these verses?

The 'focus' needed to believe God's words & live by them

OPEN THE EYES OF MY SOUL

Compare Genesis 3:1–7 with Matthew 6:22–23 and Luke 11:34–36. As you consider the purpose of the body's physical eyes, make a comparison to the soul's spiritual eyes. Look back at what we studied this week or quote any scriptures you feel support your comments.

_____
_____

Slowly read through all of John 9. Use the space below to note when the scripture uses the words "eyes," "see," "sight," or "blind."

Eyes	Sight	See	Blind

I love that John 9:1 says, "He (Jesus) saw a man who was blind from birth." Jesus didn't just notice the blind man's physical state. He looked at his spiritual condition. How sweet that Jesus' concern for us is the inward condition of our souls! Praise Him for seeing past our outward appearance and into our hearts!

In verses 1–12, what did Jesus do to open the eyes of the blind man, and why is this significant? How has Jesus removed spiritual blindness in your life?

Spit - made mud - put on blind man's eyes - Wash in pool of Siloam - blind man could see - due to faith in Jesus' word. Obey

Did you notice how the blind man obeyed before he could see? That is faith!

_____
_____

Hidden Treasures

As the brain is the control board for the human sensory system, Jesus is the head of the body of Christ in which all power resides.

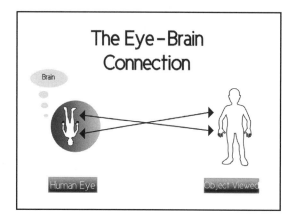

Every image viewed through the eyes is seen upside down. Our intelligent, God-given brain flips the image so that we perceive the figure correctly. This incredible act takes place through the **optic nerve,** which transmits visual information from the back of the eye to the brain. God is amazing!

What has the Lord taught you about the way He wired our eyes to our brain? Think about the way this process can also apply to your spiritual eyes, and write your thoughts below so that you can share with others in the group.

_____
_____
_____
_____

Celebrating Treasured Gifts

Are you in a situation where you need Jesus to help you view things in a whole different way? Maybe your marriage isn't meeting your expectations or you are experiencing turmoil in your church. Possibly your child is rebellious toward the Lord and you feel God isn't answering your prayers. Whatever your situation, journal your feelings and ask the Lord to show you His plan.

_____
_____
_____
_____

OPEN THE EYES OF MY SOUL

Reflection Pause

When we look at the world through spiritual eyes, it is like viewing an optical illusion. We are confused and can't understand why life events happen the way they do. But as believers in Jesus Christ, we can interpret things based on our relationship with Him.

Take another look at the illustration of the eye-brain connection. Insert "Jesus" for the word "brain," "man" for "eye," and "the world" for "the image."

Examine a real-life scenario. A man is fired from his job. He has a family of six to feed, and his situation is very grim. He knows in his heart that his co-worker set him up. Anger and bitterness are establishing residence in his heart. But when he turns to Jesus for guidance, he begins to see that God does have a plan for him. As a result, his relationship with Jesus strengthens, he is a witness to those around him, and ultimately God is glorified!

Ask the Lord to help you view your life circumstances through Jesus' eyes so you might understand the image He sees, not the optical illusion you see.

"The eye is the lamp of the body" (Matt. 6:22).

WEEK 3: DAY 2

A TOUCH TO THE SOUL

Someone touched me; I know that power has gone out from me.

—Luke 8:46

Take a step back in time. Do you remember as a child playing a game where you were blindfolded and given bowls containing different foods? As you slowly inserted your hand into each container, you tried to name the items. I remember touching cooked spaghetti, peeled grapes, Jell-O®, and some other interesting things. It always amazed me when I guessed the bowl's contents just by feeling them.

God used this silly kid's game to teach me a wonderful life lesson about the gift of touch. Ask Him to teach you through today's lesson on "A Touch of the Soul."

Please close your eyes and touch the different things within your reach. You can feel the differences in soft or coarse fabrics, the ridged edges of a pencil, hot and cold beverages, the contour of an item, etc. This touch sensation in the body is called the "tactile system," and it is the largest part of the sensory system. This system is experienced through the largest organ of the body: the skin. As the skin is affected by different stimuli, pulses travel through the body by means of the nervous system. In a split second, a touch is transmitted to the brain for decoding. Wow, we truly are an amazing machine created by the most incredible designer: God!

Real Life Facts[7]

- The sense of touch is more refined than any device ever created.
- The skin is the largest organ of the body.
- On an average adult, the skin weighs 11 kg or about 24 lbs.
- Every month a new layer replaces the entire outer surface of the skin.
- The skin has an average of three million sweat glands.

Scripture Excavation

Again we start our study reading Genesis. Read Genesis 2:16–17 and Genesis 3:1–6. What did Eve add in Genesis 3:3 that is not in Genesis 2:16–17? Why do you think she added this statement in her conversation with the serpent?

Tree of good & evil - Eve said tree in middle of garden

Look again at verse 6. After Eve saw the forbidden tree, what did she do before taking a bite of the fruit?

Saw it as food - pleasing to the eye & gaining wisdom -

In Day 1, Jesus exhibited mercy, grace, and love as He healed a man who was blind from birth. Today as we focus on "A Touch to the Soul," read Luke 8:40–56.

There are basically two stories intertwined within these scriptures: Jairus' daughter restored to life (Luke 8:40–42, 49–56) and the woman with bleeding (Luke 8:43–48). What is significant about each story and why are they interwoven within this same block of scripture?

They both believed.

Use one word to describe Jesus' teaching to the father, the woman, the disciples, and the crowd. Explain your answer. *Faith*

Turn your attention to the bleeding woman. Not one physician could heal her ongoing female problem. For twelve years she spent all her money on doctors, medicines, and natural remedies with no results. Because of her condition, she became an outcast to society, and she lived a very lonely existence. She experienced physical exhaustion from her loss of blood. Through pure willpower she gathered enough strength to get out of bed and stagger her way through the throng of people to reach her last hope: Jesus. The moment her fingers touched the edge of His cloak, His healing power entered her body and restored her to complete health. What a personal encounter with the Great Physician, Jesus!

5 Love Languages: A Touch to the Soul

What do you think this hopeless woman felt the moment she sensed Jesus' healing touch?

Joy

Look at Luke 8:48. What healed the woman?

her faith

Now turn your attention to Jairus and his daughter. Summarize their situation. What was lacking in Jairus' spiritual life? Give verses to support your opinion.

Read verses 47 and 54–55 again, and list the similarities and differences of these two accounts. Why are these significant to Jesus' teaching to the people involved and to those observing?

Most of the time I resist the urge to share my answers with you, but I must express my thoughts at this point. Consider this idea: After the *eyes* are set on a sin, the *touch* of the sin is experienced. For example, a toddler relates to the sense of touch. When he or she touches a soft blanket, he or she feels the world's warmth. But when he places his hand on a hot stove, he finds out pain is a consequence of disobedience.

This was also true with Adam and Eve. She fixed her eyes on obtaining wisdom from eating the fruit of the tree, but the act of grabbing the fruit, bringing it to her mouth and Adam taking a bite opened the door for sin to enter the world forever. From this point forward, man is born into a fallen world, with a sin nature. Praise God, He sent Jesus, His only Son, to redeem those of us who confess Jesus as Lord of our lives. Jesus' personal touch will change a person's soul forever.

Now consider this statement: When our eyes are set on Jesus, we experience His touch. Amen!

Hidden Treasures

When you study the Word, it is imperative to consider the entire context of the scripture. You should note the author, the audience, to whom the message is written, when it was written, and so on. In this case, move forward to Luke 9:1. What is the first word of the chapter?

When

Why are the words "then" or "when" used at the beginning of a verse?

Read Luke 9:1–6. Why did Luke use this transitional word? Why was it important for Jesus' disciples to witness the miracles in Luke 8?

_____

_____

Throughout Jesus' three-year ministry, He repeatedly used life situations to teach His disciples. Why? Because the disciples needed to grasp everything about Jesus: His grace and mercy, salvation through Him alone, His power, His unconditional love, His precepts, His purposes, His authority, and that He died for all. These disciples were chosen to carry on the message of salvation through Jesus to the world after His death, resurrection, and ascension. Read Matthew 28:16–20, the Great Commission. They were to "make disciples of all nations," and we are commissioned to accomplish this as well. What a privilege it is to partner with Jesus and the disciples as messengers of the gospel!

Celebrating Treasured Gifts

One night my niece and her friends gathered at my mom and dad's house for a slumber party. Like all high school girls, they talked for hours about the same things. Then a couple of the girls ventured out to the back yard to sit under the gazebo. A dim light illuminated the area as the girls continued in deep conversation. All of a sudden, a gentle hand grasped one of the girls' shoulder. As she turned around, she immediately realized the eyes looking at her were not human! For a split second, she thought an alien from another planet had invaded and grabbed her—but then she realized that a raccoon was perched on the back of her lounge chair.

The girls screamed in fright as they ran toward the house. Dad headed out the back door like Superman showing up to save the day. Catching their breath, the girls explained the cause of their fright. At once, laughter filled the house as they reenacted the event over and over. What an example of the way an unexpected touch can affect someone in an unusual way!

Journal your thoughts about something special you learned today. Compare and contrast how physical touch affects the body and Jesus' spiritual touch affects the soul. It is a known fact—if a person writes down his thoughts, he or she is much more likely to remember them. Therefore, journal away!

_____

_____

Reflection Pause

What tender lessons did Jesus teach through His miracle of healing the woman who touched his cloak? To begin with, Jesus' touch allowed the woman a personal encounter with the Great Physician. Jesus permitted the multitude to witness this miracle so that they might understand that every individual has value. The father, Jairus, who lacked faith, experienced seeing a woman healed because of her faith. Jesus gave the crowd an opportunity to see how He loved someone whom the world viewed as a society outcast. Once again, the disciples witnessed Jesus' compassion for His people. This on-the-job training opened the way for the disciples to carry on the message of salvation to the world.

Look beyond the obvious in Scripture to discover the treasures waiting for you to behold them! Amen!

WEEK 3: DAY 3

THE TASTE OF JESUS

Taste and see that the Lord is good.

—Psalm 34:8

I can remember taking liquid medicine as a child. The initial flavor as it entered my mouth tasted sweet. Then as it coated the inside of my mouth and throat, the nerves in my face began to constrict. This caused an uncontrollable contorted look to appear on my face! That bitter taste seemed to last all day long. In fact, as I think about it right now, my mouth puckers and I still taste it!

You probably remember tasting something similar, or possibly you were the mom watching your child's face pucker up. This reminds me of life—when we allow bitter situations, attitudes, or relationships to linger, they will affect every area of our lives. When a root of bitterness grows in our hearts, it influences our attitudes, actions, language, relationships, appearance, and more. Get rid of any bitterness before it takes root!

How do you decide what to eat for breakfast? Do you wake up craving something sweet, like a doughnut or maybe yogurt with fruit and granola? Maybe you yearn for the taste of something salty, like an egg and bacon burrito. Have you ever thought about why foods taste different?

God created our tongues with thousands of tiny taste buds that cover not only the tongue but also, for a time, the roof of the mouth. Tasting is an amazing process! In a nutshell, as you eat, the saliva in your mouth helps break down the food, and that activates receptor cells located in your taste buds. These receptors send messages to the brain, and in turn, the brain recognizes the flavors you taste.

Real Life Facts.[8]

- We have thousands of taste buds inside our mouths.
- Humans make 1,000 to 1,500 milliliters of saliva a day.
- Taste buds are actually tiny nerve endings that reproduce every ten days.
- Food entering the mouth activates the saliva glands.

God creatively equipped a human's tongue to taste four basic kinds of flavors: sweet, salty, sour, and bitter. Observe this diagram. Notice the salty/sweet taste buds located in the front section of the tongue. The sour taste buds are positioned on each side of the tongue, and bitter taste buds are located in the far back. The middle section has very few taste buds. Everyone's tastes vary and, in fact, change as they get older. A baby not only has taste buds on his or her tongue, but also on the roof and sides of his or her mouth. As the child ages, the taste buds on the roof and sides of the mouth slowly disappear, leaving only those on the tongue. The remaining taste buds become less sensitive, allowing him or her to eat foods that seemed too strong when he or she was a child.

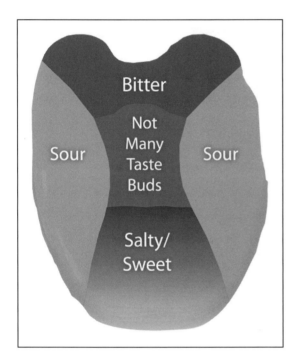

Now, this is going to be fun! Meditate on what you read in the previous paragraph, along with the verse at the beginning of today's lesson: "Oh, taste and see that the Lord is good." Think back to your "baby" Christian days, those fresh and new experiences with Jesus when you were like a baby with a mouth full of taste buds. Reading the Bible reminded you of a child on Christmas morning—it compared to opening a beautifully-wrapped gift. Maybe as time passed, your life became busy and you began neglecting your daily quiet time with the Lord. As a result, your Christian walk dulled, like an adult who has lost sensitivity in his or her taste buds. As you experienced sour things in life, you were left with a bitter taste in your mouth. Then at some point, because of Jesus' love for you, He gave you a taste of something so sweet about Himself that it left you craving for more of Him. In addition, He salted an area of your life that caused you to thirst again for the living water that only He can provide. "Oh, taste and see that the Lord is good" today through your lesson!

Scripture Excavation

We read about the physical characteristics of our taste buds. Now let's move to some spiritual lessons and examine how God uses similes in the Bible for *sweet, salty, sour* and *bitter*. Ask the Holy Spirit to speak to you through this lesson.

THE TASTE OF JESUS

As you read Genesis 3:1–6, jot down what happened the moment Eve tasted the fruit.
_____
_____

Spiritually, what happens the minute you take a taste of sin? How does it taste at first? What happens if the taste lingers?
_____
_____

Use the analogy of eating only potato chips all day, every day. What nutritional value would they give your physical body? Parallel this to what happens when, as a believer in Jesus, you don't spend time in prayer, reading the Bible, worshipping God, or interacting with other believers.
_____
_____

Let's look at the four areas of the tongue and see what we can learn from them:

1. Sweet taste buds:

Read Ezekiel 3:1–3. What is Ezekiel to do with the scroll and why?
_____
_____

Share a time when you experienced the sweetness of Scripture. What happened as a result?
_____
_____

2. Salty taste buds:

Read Matthew 5:13, Mark 9:49–50, and Luke 14:34–35. What did you learn about salt from these three passages? What are some of the uses of salt? If possible, use different scriptures to back up your answers.
_____
_____

When you eat salty foods, what happens to your body? How does food with too much salt taste?
_____
_____

3. Sour taste buds:

Read Proverbs 10:26. Vinegar is basically a liquid that has soured. In biblical times, vinegar was usually made from water poured over pressed grapes. After sitting for a while, the mixture fermented into sour-tasting liquid called vinegar. Look back at the diagram and notice where the sour taste buds are located. Now explain your thoughts about this verse.

_____
_____

4. Bitter taste buds:

The Greek root word for bitterness is *pikria,* which means bitter gall, extreme wickedness, a bitter root, producing a bitter fruit, and bitter hatred. Read Hebrews 12:14–17. What does a root of bitterness do to a person? Can you give examples in Scripture?

_____
_____

Remember where the bitter taste buds are located? They are situated on the back of the tongue, next to the sour taste buds and before the esophagus, which ends at the stomach. Everything you eat must pass over the bitter taste buds. Apply this physical condition to the spiritual life.

_____
_____

Hidden Treasures

For the final scripture today, read James 3:1–12, noting all the references to the tongue. Journal your thoughts and what the Lord is conveying to you through this scripture.

_____
_____

Now focus on verses 11 and 12. What are the two tastes referenced, and what do you think is the purpose for this analogy?

_____
_____

THE TASTE OF JESUS

Celebrating Treasured Gifts

What is the Lord teaching you today about the sense of taste? Have you learned anything new to enhance your daily walk with Jesus? Write down your praises, thoughts, and prayers. Be ready to share these with the group.

_____

_____

_____

_____

_____

_____

Reflection Pause

Salt and sugar look similar. How easy would it be to mistake one for the other, to reach for the wrong ingredient? Can you imagine tasting a cake with one cup of salt instead of one cup of sugar? I'd spit it out quickly! As Christians, if we allow the world to guide our choices, we end up with the salt and sugar comparison. Things may look the same from the outside, but in reality, they are opposites. As we study the Word, we begin to view things from God's perspective. We not only *see* but also *feel* the texture, *taste* the difference, and *hear* His warnings when situations are not as they seem. Experience "The Taste of Jesus" daily so you can tell what is real!

WEEK 3: DAY 4

THE AROMA OF CHRIST

For we are to God the aroma of Christ.

—2 Corinthians 2:15

Recently my son opened the kitchen pantry door and loudly yelled, "Mom, there is something in here that stinks!" When I entered the pantry, the fumes were so strong that I thought I would throw up. Holding my breath, I searched for the source of the repulsive smell. My groping hands finally landed in something wet on the floor, and I found the source of the smell: a bag of potatoes. As I moved the bag, it reeked with a stench so nauseating that I ran, gagging, out of the pantry. The odor that had been confined to the shut-up space quickly followed me through the door and into the kitchen. One rotten potato affected the whole bag! By this time, my other children had entered the kitchen. As I turned around to show them the evidence, they all ran away, leaving me with the stinky mess.

Thinking about the incident later, I realized an odor has the power to draw people to it or send them running. It is worthy to note that the same kitchen pantry is where I bake homemade bread. When the bread is baking, the wonderful smell lures my children to the pantry with their mouths watering. It is such a blessing to provide delicious anticipation before they ever take a bite of the bread!

Notice in both situations, the kitchen pantry didn't produce either aroma. The processes taking place inside the pantry generated the smells. This could also be a picture of us as Christians. We are the pantry, and what is produced within us will either draw people to Jesus or turn them away. Have fun today as you study "The Aroma of Jesus"!

God created humans with the amazing ability to detect thousands of odors. This automatic sense of smell, called the olfactory system, is constantly activated in our bodies. Because of this high level of sensitivity, we are able to distinguish between smells that draw us to the source, and odors that cause us to run away. Imagine walking through the mall when the scent of freshly brewed coffee captures your attention. Immediately, the desire for a satisfying cappuccino enters your mind. Many times this savory aroma lingers in your brain until the desire is satisfied. On the other hand, some odors are considered a stench instead of a pleasant scent. For example, you might be driving your car when you smell something horrible. All it takes is one whiff for you to know you ran over or came too close to a skunk. Within seconds, everyone complains about the stink.

What causes some smells to be pleasant and some to be foul? How does the olfactory system operate? Prepare your heart to hear from the Lord today!

Real Life Facts[9]

- Hairs in the nose help to warm and clean the air we breathe.
- The highest recorded "sneeze speed" is 165 kilometers per hour.
- A person at rest usually breathes between twelve and fifteen times a minute.
- At rest, the adult body takes in and breathes out about six liters of air each minute.
- An adult's sense of smell is less sensitive than a child's.

Scripture Excavation

Again let's look at some passages of Scripture in the book of Genesis. Read Genesis 2:4–17 with 3:1–7. Think about what it must have been like to walk in the Garden of Eden in its perfect state before sin entered the world. Write a brief explanation of the fragrances Adam and Eve might have inhaled and the effects from them.

_____

_____

How might the fragrances have changed the minute sin entered the world?

_____

_____

In biblical times, sweet perfumes and odors were used to reflect triumphs and victories. Conversely, there were fragrances that represented death. In the passage above, Paul used the Roman triumphal procession as a figure of speech to praise God. In a victory procession, the priests followed the Roman general with vessels filled with incense. This allowed the spectators to smell the odor of victory over the enemy. Paul, of course, presents God as the conquering general leading the victory parade. He and the others who preached about

THE AROMA OF CHRIST

Jesus released the sweet fragrance of victory in Christ. The name *Jesus* in the Greek means "the anointed one," "salvation," "Messiah."[10] In other words, His anointing is a sweet aroma that penetrates everything and everyone. As Jesus indwells believers, His fragrance seeps out from us to those we encounter.

Read 2 Corinthians 2:14–17. The Greek word for "fragrance" is *euodia,* which means a fragrant or sweet smelling thing, incense, an odor. Metaphorically speaking, it denotes something well-pleasing to God. In light of these definitions, what is this passage saying to you personally?

_____
_____

Who is the aroma of Christ to God?

_____
_____

It is very important never to take scriptures out of context. Therefore, after reading this whole passage again, what is its focus? Who gets the credit and why? What is the purpose in all of it?

_____
_____

Hidden Treasures

Let's dig a little deeper and look at what God has to say about breath. Look back at Genesis 2:7. What does it say God did to man after He formed him?

_____
_____

Give an explanation of what you think *breath of life* means, not only from a physical aspect but also from a spiritual viewpoint.

_____
_____

Now rest for a moment and take a deep breath, allowing your lungs to fill to capacity. Close your eyes and exhale slowly. What does oxygen do for the physical body?

_____
_____

If the air supply is restricted, what happens?

_____
_____

Compare the analogy above to what happens to your soul when you spend time with Jesus everyday. Remember our "soul balloon" comparison? With that in mind, explain this statement: "To breathe in the freshness of Jesus daily keeps my soul filled with completeness."

_____
_____

Celebrating Treasured Gifts

"Thank You, God, for everything You have shown me today about . . ."

_____
_____
_____
_____
_____
_____

Reflection Pause

All the Christmas decorations are strategically placed in the house. The outside lights are shining brightly, and a chill is in the air. My daughter, Carly, walked into the kitchen and said, "Mom, why doesn't it feel like Christmas?" I thought about her heartfelt question throughout the day, and I purchased a candle called "Christmas Tradition." After arriving home, I lit the new candle and placed it on the kitchen counter. Immediately, the smell of Christmas filled the air. When Carly came home later that afternoon, I heard her proclaim, "Mom, I love that smell! Now it feels like Christmas!"

How did the aroma of the candle affect her feeling of Christmas? Why didn't the Christmas decor and lights bring about this emotion? Could this be like the Christian life? We allow things often regarded as Christian accessories to replace Christ's inward aroma. Wearing Christian t-shirts or jewelry will not create a deeper relationship with Jesus. It is when we "breathe" Him in that we experience Jesus' aroma, an intimate relationship that is sweet and tender.

"Therefore, be imitators of God as dearly loved children. And walk in love, as Christ also loved us and gave Himself for us, an offering and a sacrifice to God for a sweet-smelling aroma" (Eph. 5:1–2).

WEEK 3: DAY 5

EARS TO HEAR

My sheep hear My voice.

—John 10:27 NKJV

We have come to the end of our study on "Senses of the Soul." My prayer is that you are convinced that only Jesus satisfies the senses of touch, aroma, taste, sight, and sound of the soul. Think back on all you studied this week. Has your relationship with Christ been enriched? Today, prepare to learn from the Lord as you dive into "Ears to Hear."

Have you ever heard a noise in the dark that caused fear to immediately envelop your whole body? The scenario could go something like this: It is 11:30 p.m. You are lying in bed, almost asleep, in a pitch-black room. All of a sudden, you hear a noise at the window, and your imagination begins to run wild. Shivering, you listen again for the suspicious noise. You wait a minute—the sound is less intrusive, but still there. Throwing the covers off, you run to turn on the light. A feeling of instant comfort comes over you as light fills the room. To your surprise, when you peek out the window you notice a branch blowing wildly in the wind, scratching against the window. Relief immediately replaces the fear in your heart.

What is it about hearing things in the dark that can take us to a place of worry, trembling, and unrealistic thoughts? Are you in a spiritually dark place in your life? Are noises and voices pouring into your head, gripping you with fear, guilt, anxiety, and hopelessness? Just like getting out of your bed to turn on the light, you can get out of your dark place and run to the light of Christ. Believe and know that He is waiting for you to fall into His secure and loving arms.

The sense of hearing is an amazing and complex part of the body. I remember my first pregnancy. Many of the books I read said if you read to your infant in the womb, he or she would be a brighter child. Moreover, if you listen to classical music during the nine months of development, he definitely will be more intelligent. I thought, *That's crazy! How can a baby hear from inside the womb?* But as a first time mother, I didn't want to miss an opportunity to impart wisdom to my child. So off and running, I went with these baby book ideas. Despite my skepticism, I started reading a children's Christian book out loud almost every day to the baby in my womb. To my amazement, as he grew and started choosing his favorite books for me to read, that little book continued to be the number one choice!

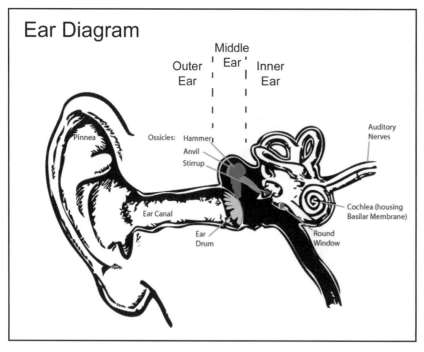

Real Life Facts

The human ear is the mechanism used to collect sounds, process them, and send signals about them to the brain for decoding. The ear is made up of three different sections: the outer ear, the middle ear, and the inner ear. These parts all work together so you can hear and process sounds. Another very important responsibility of the ear is to help keep the body in balance so that when you bend over to pick up something from the floor you won't fall down.

The outer ear's main job is to collect sounds from outside the body. It also produces wax, which coats the ear canal and helps fight infections. Once sound waves are collected, they travel through the ear canal to the middle ear, where they are turned into vibrations. These vibrations are then funneled to the inner ear, where a number of hair-like cells are waiting to transmit signals to the brain for translation. This all happens within a split second! Be prepared to hear what the Lord has planned for you as you work your way through "Ears to Hear."

EARS TO HEAR

Scripture Excavation

Read Genesis 3:1–7. To whom did Eve listen while she walked in the Garden of Eden, and what should she have done when she heard the words that were spoken?

_____

_____

Now read Genesis 3:8–13. It says in verse 8, "Then the man and his wife heard the sound of the Lord God." They didn't see God—they heard God. What did they hear?

_____

_____

Why is it important to test and examine everything you hear against God's Word? For answers to this question, turn to the New Testament and read 1 John 4:1–6. Give solid answers from this and other scriptures that come to mind.

_____

_____

The apostle John knew God called him to proclaim Jesus Christ's message to the world. From the 1 John scripture above, write down all the references to the words "heard" and "listen." What is John proclaiming to have heard?

_____

_____

Hidden Treasures

Would you like to hear God talking to you, to actually hear His voice? I've always thought it would be so much easier if God spoke out loud so that I could understand Him. That way I wouldn't second-guess Him or try to figure out what He really means. This is a great discussion question. Write your thoughts.

_____

_____

Refer to the diagram of the ear. Think back on the scriptures today. How could the physical ear's functions be used to explain spiritually hearing God's Word? Really ask the Lord to help you go beyond the obvious and grab hold of a life-changing lesson!

_____

_____

REFLECTING HIM

Do you agree with the definitions below? Write your thoughts, and have fun with your answers!

- Outer ear—Hearing the world around me
- Middle ear—Processing what I hear
- Inner ear—Transmitting information to the brain; balancing God's Word
- Brain—Internalizing the final results

_____

_____

Finally, read Isaiah 40:12. Remember, another function of the inner ear is to maintain balance. What is God saying to you through this verse?

_____

_____

As the inner ear gives you physical balance, God's Word gives you spiritual balance. When you hear a statement "in the name of Jesus," make sure to compare the information to what God says in His Word. We are warned in 2 Peter 2 of false teachers and their destructive doctrines. Check everything to make sure it lines up with what the whole Bible has to say. When statements are taken out of context or only part of a passage is used, God's Word can become distorted. That is why, in my opinion, a personal study of God's Word is vital to your spiritual growth. It helps you to become deeply grounded in your faith. My husband has read through the whole Bible at least six times. He says through this process, God opened his eyes to the way the whole Bible is totally interlinked from Genesis to Revelation. The Holy Spirit is waiting for us to dive into the Word so that He can make known God's promises and wisdom (see 1 Cor. 2:13). Aren't you thankful God gave us two ears to balance, not just one!

Celebrating Treasured Gifts

Take time right now to hear what God is saying to you. Process it! Balance it! Transmit it! Allow your soul to internalize what God is showing you about Himself. Journal your thoughts and soul on the lines of this page as you celebrate the treasured gifts God showed you this week about the "Senses of the Soul."

_____

_____

_____

_____

_____

Reflection Pause

I must share something exciting that the Lord revealed to me while studying this passage of Scripture. In fact, I jumped out of my chair and screamed, "God you are *so* good!" This morning, God reminded me that the inner ear is where the body maintains balance. I looked up the Hebrew definition for "balance" from Isaiah 40:12. Are you ready for this? It comes from the Hebrew word *azan,* which means to hear, listen, give ear; perceived by the ear. It gives the idea of scales, as if two ears are in balance.

Think about it: God gives us two ears to hear His Word, process it, and balance it in our lives. Take time to praise God for His provisions and grace!

WEEK 4

THE POWER SOURCE: THE FATHER, THE SON, AND THE HOLY SPIRIT

For the message of the cross is foolishness to those who are perishing, but to us who are being saved it is the power of God.

—1 Corinthians 1:18

When you think of power, what comes to mind? Maybe you think of a bodybuilder lifting a barbell two times his own weight or the forceful intensity of a hurricane bearing down on a populated area. Another portrayal of power is the person with the highest position in the country—the president. No matter how the word "power" is used, there is a common thread of strength and authority.

How would you explain the word "source"? In the timber industry, for example, trees supply wood for the production of chairs, tables, beds, and couch frames. The trees are the "root" of this process. Another source is electricity. At the push of a button, electricity is waiting to supply your house with the energy to operate the air conditioner, lights, alarm system, septic tank, washer/dryer, etc. But as you well know, the electricity supply doesn't originate in the outlets, the electrical lines, or the electrical power box. It originates from a power plant. Ultimately, a *source* refers to a foundation, supplier, basis, or starting place.

Regardless of your definitions of "power" and "source," it is critical to understand that everything in the past, present, and future originates from God. In Genesis 1:3, we read that creation began at the sound of God's voice: "Let there be light." What caused the light? We know the sun didn't cause it, because the sun comes later in the creation process. This week, in our study of "The Power Source," we tackle the question of light, and search the scriptures for God's truths.

The sun is God's source to sustain life on earth. It is the physical light of the world. Everything on earth is driven by the sun's power: life cycles, photosynthesis, temperature, and radiance all provide beauty, balance the weather patterns, keep the oceans in check, and more. God sent His power to earth in the human form of Jesus to be the spiritual light of the world. God gave Him authority to forgive all sins and redeem the world through His death and resurrection. Now Jesus sits at God's right hand, interceding for those who believe in Him. The Holy Spirit indwells believers and seals them with the mark that says, "This one belongs to Jesus!" Basically, the Holy Spirit is the power connector from believers to Jesus and God.

We have some exciting things to study this week!

The Sun Light

Have you ever seen a sunrise stretching across the whole horizon? It can be a breathtaking experience. An array of colors creates a brilliant picture bursting across the break of dawn. All of a sudden, the moment of splendor grows fainter and then vanishes into the morning sky. But the image is still embedded in your mind. Questions arise: What is the power behind this spectacular display? Will this same magnificent image ever be reproduced? How did God create this brilliant sight that causes hearts to skip a beat?

Prepare yourself for another exciting study. We begin with "The Dawning Light," which examines light vs. darkness. In "Here Comes the Sun," the spotlight is on the sun's formation and its characteristics. Then we take a glance at "The Sun-Earth Connection," where the focal point is directly on the sun's rays. Next, we turn our attention to "The Sun Link," in which we concentrate on the sun sustaining all life on earth. Finally, we conclude our study with "Light Up My Life," the effects the sun has on human life. Carl Williams, a solar energy expert with more than forty years in the field, is guiding us through our study this week. Not only is he a knowledgeable chemical engineer, but also, he's my dad!

As you move through this week, my prayer is that you experience freshness in your walk with the Lord. Every morning as you see the sunrise or feel the sun's rays beaming down on your skin, I pray it's your reminder to let Jesus' light shine in your life. May you experience spiritual brightness in your life as you study "The Power Source"!

WEEK 4: DAY 1

THE DAWNING LIGHT

God . . . separated the light from the darkness.

—Genesis 1:4

About twenty years ago, an experience opened my eyes to the light vs. darkness issue. After giving birth to Jake, our second son, I suffered from one of the common aftereffects of a natural delivery: hemorrhoids! If you have ever experienced the throbbing pain of this annoying condition, you probably are empathizing with me at this very moment. A month after Jake's birth, I awakened in the middle of the night to an immense pounding pain that ignited every nerve in my body. I quietly tiptoed to the bathroom to use the medicine I knew would provide immediate relief. As a thoughtful wife, I decided not to turn on the light because it might wake up my husband, Fred. I reached into the drawer for the tube of medicine, applied it liberally, and then staggered back to bed. Not thirty seconds later, I felt a fire ignite in my lower regions. Instantly, I realized the "hemorrhoid medicine" I had used was actually a tube of Deep Heat! Like a rocket in flight, I leaped from the bed to the bathroom, turned on the coldest water in the bathtub, stepped in, and bent over—well, you probably get the picture. In the meantime, Fred, awakened by all the commotion, walked into the bathroom and turned on the light to find his wife squatting in the tub with a horrid look on her face. He probably felt he was in the middle of a nightmare. I will leave you to imagine the rest of the story.

I learned a valuable lesson that night. If I had turned on the light, I guarantee I would have picked up the correct medicine. When we try to do things in the dark, we are apt to make wrong decisions. Equate this to our daily lives—if we live in Jesus' light, He guides and helps us make the correct choices. By the way, in case you are wondering, the cold water did eventually relieve my throbbing pain, but my sweet husband continued to laugh for hours!

In Genesis 1:2–3, we read that the earth was formless and empty, darkness was over the surface of the deep, and God's Spirit was hovering over the waters. Then God said, "Let there be light," and light appeared.

Real Life Facts

Imagine a world in total darkness. Think of the world before the creation of light. Light provides us with the ability to see the life on earth that God created. It produces energy, sustains the life cycle, supplies thermal heat, and much more. Without light, the world would cease to exist as we know it. Today, may your heart be enlightened as you focus on "The Dawning Light."

Scripture Excavation

Take a minute to focus on the picture at the beginning of today's study. What thoughts run through your mind? Are you mesmerized as you focus on the center of the picture? Or is your attention drawn outward as you follow the light rays?

_____

_____

Read Genesis 1, making mental notes of the order of creation. Before you begin, ask God to show you something new about the creation story. Picture God before, during, and after the process, and journal your thoughts. Have fun with this!

_____

_____

What was the earth like in the beginning? Give your description of "total darkness."

_____

_____

Who was with God, and what was He doing?

_____

_____

THE DAWNING LIGHT

Hidden Treasures

Read Matthew 4:12–17 and Isaiah 9:1–2. In Isaiah 9:2 there are two contrasts that need to be identified. What are they, and why are they important? The prophet tried to get what point across?

_____

_____

Read Matthew 4:1–11 to get an understanding of Jesus' experience prior to the beginning of His public ministry. At that time, Jesus was about thirty years old and just had been baptized by John the Baptist. Led by the Holy Spirit into the wilderness, Jesus fasted forty days and forty nights. Immediately after Jesus' fast, while He was in a state of physical weakness, Satan tempted Jesus in every way possible. Of all the scriptures, why do you think Jesus first preached Isaiah 9:1–2?

_____

_____

Celebrating Treasured Gifts

Today, take a moment to look outside. Notice how natural light allows you to see the contrasting colors in your yard, birds flittering from one place to another, or clouds creating incredible images in the sky. Take time to thank God for the physical light of His creation, and praise Him for the spiritual light of Jesus. "I am the light of the world. Whoever follows me will never walk in darkness, but will have the light of life" (John 8:12).

_____

_____

_____

_____

_____

Reflection Pause

We must take a moment to reflect on a few things. Think of what this phrase is really saying: "God said. . . ." Consider this for a moment: As God breathed out the words, "Let there be light," light came into existence out of the darkness. Does this give you confidence in the Lord or what? I love the next phrase: "and there was light." It could have been said like this: "Of course there was light, because what God says will be!" Oh, the power of God's Word!

The sun had yet to be created, so what was the light? I truly believe the beginning of creation is symbolic of God's purpose for all human life. The earth was without form, dark, empty, and void of beauty until God breathed light into existence. In a like manner, the human soul exists as a state of confusion, disorder, and spiritual darkness. But when a person believes in the Lord Jesus Christ, immediately the light of Christ is breathed into his or her soul. Someone who once could not understand the things of God shines with Christ's light forevermore. Oh, how the vision of a soul newly marked with the Holy Spirit's seal must bring a smile to God's face!

WEEK 4: DAY 2

HERE COMES THE SON!

God made two great lights—the greater light to govern the day and the lesser light to govern the night.
—Genesis 1:16

As a child, do you remember experiencing your first eclipse of the sun? I recall my first grade class venturing outside to observe this spectacular event. We each were handed two pieces of paper: one regular sheet and the other with a small hole punched through the middle of the page. Why? Because when a person looks directly at the sun with unprotected eyes, the sun can permanently damage that person's vision. So we turned our backs to the sun and held up the paper with the hole in it. Soon the image flowed through the hole onto the other piece of paper, allowing us to watch the eclipse on paper without damaging our eyesight.

What makes the sun so powerful? To grasp its power, we must first understand a few of its characteristics. This huge, glowing ball of gas is located right in the center of our solar system. Everything in our solar system, including the nine planets and their moons and billions of asteroids and trillions of comets, revolves around the sun. Gravitational attraction holds the gases together and produces immense pressure and massive temperatures at its core. This stationary radiant sphere provides the earth with the light, heat, and energy it needs to survive. Moreover, it energizes photosynthesis in green plants, and is the ultimate source for all food and fossil fuel. The way the sun and earth interact drives the seasons, ocean currents, weather, and climate.

The sun is enormous! One way to grasp its mass is to compare the sun to the earth. If the earth's radius were the width of a sewing needle, the sun's diameter would be approximately the height of a regular kitchen table. It's almost too hard to comprehend!

Real Life Facts[11]

- It takes an average of eight minutes for the sun's rays to reach the earth.
- The earth is located about ninety-three million miles from the sun.
- The sun's radius is about 109 times the radius of the earth.
- The temperature of the surface we see is about 5,500 degrees Celsius.
- The sun is a ball of gas consisting mainly of hydrogen and helium.

The sun seems too far away to affect the earth's surface. But have you ever experienced the excruciating pain of a sunburn? How does this happen from a source millions of miles away? Let's look at the sun's characteristics and compare them to the traits of Jesus, the Son of God.

Scripture Excavation

Go back to Genesis 1:14–19. What do you learn about the sun from these scriptures? Be very specific!

_____

_____

Let's do a word search on "great lights" from Genesis 1:16. Find the original Hebrew meaning for these words. If you don't have a *Strong's Concordance*, search online for a Web site that will help you discover these meanings:

- Great

_____

_____

- Lights

_____

_____

With these definitions in mind, read Psalm 136:1–9 along with the Genesis verses. What do you learn about God from these verses?

_____

_____

HERE COMES THE SON!

Prepare for your heart to skip a beat as you read Psalm 19. From this chapter, assemble a few comparisons between the sun and the Son of God, Jesus. This is a challenging question, so ask the Holy Spirit to open your spiritual eyes to His teachings.

_____

_____

The Sun	Jesus

The Hebrew definition of "sun" is *shemesh*, which most often refers to the celestial body that illuminates the Earth. Biblically speaking, the sun is symbolic of righteousness. In Psalm 84:11, the sun is even used as a title for God. In ancient times, many people worshipped the sun, moon, and stars. But it is clear that the psalmist understood that the sun, moon, and stars worshipped the Creator who made them: God.

Hidden Treasures

Let's look at a couple of specific physical characteristics of the sun and make a spiritual analogy to Jesus, the Son of God. My prayer is that each time you see the brilliance of a sunrise, view the radiance of a sunset, or experience the brightness of the light of day, you are reminded of Jesus as the Light of the World.

Temperature

Physical: As stated in the Real Life Facts, the sun's surface has a temperature of about 5,500 degrees Celsius. That would fry an egg while still inside the hen! The earth is perfectly positioned to the sun to withstand the heat.

Spiritual: "For the Lord God is a sun and shield; the Lord bestows favor and honor; no good thing does he withhold from those whose walk is blameless" (Ps. 84:11). Think about this verse. How does it apply to the physical sun?

_____

_____

Gravitational Pull

Physical: The solar system is held together by the sun's gravitational pull. This phenomenon causes the planets, asteroids, comets, and dust in our solar system to be strongly attracted to the sun. This gravitational attraction keeps these bodies in orbit around the sun.

Spiritual: Jesus has spiritual gravitational pull. He said in John 12:32, "But I, when I am lifted up from the earth, will draw all men to myself." Make a comparison with the physical sun.

Position

Physical: In our solar system, earth is the third planet from the sun. Because of this position, our planet has the perfect environment for life to exist. The planets closer to the sun, such as Mercury and Venus, are too hot, while others farther away from the sun have temperatures too cold to sustain life.

Spiritual: earth is in the perfect position as the third planet from the sun; God in His perfect timing raised Jesus from the depths of the earth on the third day. Oh, sister-friend, look for God's spiritual analogies in the physical things on earth as He reveals Himself through His creation!

Celebrating Treasured Gifts

We uncovered some exciting truths today! As you conclude today's study, read John 1:1–9. Write a thank You note to God for what He personally revealed to you through this study and for Jesus, the true Light of the World.

Reflection Pause

Jesus said, "I am the Light of the World." How do you view these words from Jesus after studying "Here Comes the Son"? Remember the question at the beginning of today's lesson? What makes the sun so powerful? Through our study we discovered a variety of characteristics about its force and energy. One of its main traits is it's located in the center of the universe. Everything revolves around it. If the sun is ever removed from that position, life will cease to exist. The sun is what keeps everything in order.

What happens when you become the center of your world? When God's Son is removed from the core position in your life and you become the center of your world, does chaos take over? Are you out of order? As your world revolves around you, do you feel a cold confusion replace the warmth you once experienced?

Remember to leave Jesus in the center of your life. Revolve around Him so you experience the Son's warmth!

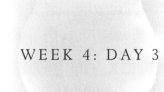

WEEK 4: DAY 3

THE SUN-EARTH CONNECTION

His splendor was like the sunrise; rays flashed from his hand, where his power was hidden.
—Habakkuk 3:4

It's just one of those days! You know, the kind that hasn't gone according to plan. As the day continues to unfold, negative thoughts invade your mind. Before you know it, those thoughts become hurtful words that start flowing like a river from your mouth. On your drive home, you realize it is much later than you thought, which means the elegant dinner you planned to cook will have to wait until another time. Once again, fast food will have to do.

All of a sudden, your car reaches the top of a hill, and your mouth drops open. In front of you is a scene that immediately penetrates the depths of your soul. A view of the sunset, in all its brilliance, blankets your heart with warmth from God. It's as if God wrote you a message that says, "Be still, My child. Rest in Me! I planned this blessing for you today. Look at the colors I painted so vividly for you to observe. Don't miss Me in your moments of frustration. I want you to experience the beauty of My creation right now!"

As tears run down your face, you realize that you did not spent any time with God that day—not a prayer, a praise, or even one thought about God. You immediately ask for forgiveness as a song of praise streams from your lips. The beauty cast before you in the sky now resonates in your heart.

REFLECTING HIM

How do we get to that point where we recognize everything is about God? Today, ask the Holy Spirit to be your teacher as you study "The Sun-Earth Connection."

Scripture Excavation

"His splendor was like the sunrise; rays flashed from his hand, where his power was hidden" (Hab. 3:4).

Read Habakkuk 3. What does the Lord show you through these verses, especially verse 4?

_____

_____

Slowly read Isaiah 48:12–19 so you can absorb each verse. Share your thoughts on these areas:

God as Creator (v. 12)

_____

_____

God Omnipotent (All-Powerful) (vv. 13–14)

_____

_____

Who is "him" and what is his mission? (v.15)

_____

_____

Who is speaking in the quote? (v. 16)

_____

_____

What is the message? (vv. 17–19)

_____

_____

Compare the verse in Habakkuk with the Isaiah passage. Ask the Holy Spirit to open your heart to learn some profound lessons He is waiting to impart to you today. Share your thoughts.

_____

_____

THE SUN-EARTH CONNECTION

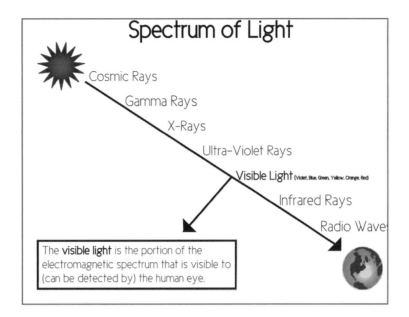

Hidden Treasures

Observe the Spectrum of Light chart. It illustrates sunlight as it travels through space to the earth in about eight minutes! As mentioned earlier, the distance between the sun and earth is about ninety-three million miles (Real Life Facts, Week 4: Day 2). This is almost too difficult for the human mind to comprehend!

The only part of the spectrum of light we see is visible light. Without a full understanding of light, it might be easy to conclude that light refers only to what you can see with your own eyes. But with this limited view you would miss the truth about the sun-to-earth light process. Notice all the other elements that are not seen: cosmic rays, gamma rays, x-rays, ultraviolet rays, infrared rays, and radio waves. If you decided to define light based on what is seen, you would never know the full power of light!

Transfer this analysis to Jesus as the sun and you as the earth. The Lord gives you the blessing of being able to see some of the things He is doing in your life. But look at how much more He is involved in the unseen. If you base the active role Jesus plays in your life on your physical circumstances and life situations, or on what you see, you miss the reality of what He is doing behind the scenes.

What insights are you learning from these verses and the Spectrum of Light chart? How can you apply these to your daily life?

_____

_____

Celebrating Treasured Gifts

Take time to praise God for the unseen things He is doing for you. Think about a circumstance in your life right now. How are you viewing this situation—through what is seen or what is unseen? Do you trust God's hand on your life? Take time to write down your thoughts, prayers, and praises about this situation.

_____

_____

_____

_____

_____

_____

_____

Reflection Pause

God has something special for us to glean from these verses. By God's hand the foundations of the earth were formed, His right hand spread out the heavens, and rays flashed from His hand—where His power was hidden. What power was hidden? Are you ready for this? Hebrews 10:12 says that after Jesus died on the cross, He ascended and sat at God's right hand. Could it be Jesus is the power that went out from God's hand to be the light of the world (see John 1:1–5; 8:12; Is. 49)? In my opinion, I shout with excitement, "Yes! Praise you, Father God, for sending Jesus to light up our lives!"

From everything we studied about light, we know that physical light affects the earth's physical existence. Likewise, Jesus affects all of the earth's spiritual existence. Picture God opening His hand so that Jesus is released to pass quickly through the universe and embed Himself in the womb of a young girl named Mary. The Light of the World was concealed in the darkness of the womb until He came into this world as a baby. At that instant, a star appeared in the eastern sky as a spotlight on the arrival of the long-awaited Messiah.

Oh, sister-friend, recognize the active hand of God in your life today, and allow Him to be the Light of your life!

WEEK 4: DAY 4

THE SUN LINK

But blessed is the man who trusts in the Lord, whose confidence is in him. He will be like a tree planted by the water that sends out its roots by the stream. It does not fear when heat comes; its leaves are always green.

—Jeremiah 17:7–8

This week in our study of "The Power Source," we surged through the analogies of light vs. darkness, the sun's powerful design, and God's hand in the sun-earth connection. Today we concentrate on the way the sun sustains the earth's life cycle. We focus on two essential areas for life on earth: photosynthesis and the water cycle. Ask the Lord to help you grasp a new perspective of how He sustains spiritual life on earth.

REFLECTING HIM

Real Life Facts

Photosynthesis is the process by which green plants take the light energy from the sun and convert it into a storable form known as glucose. Chlorophyll, which sits in the leaves of the green plants, absorbs the sunlight and converts water, carbon dioxide, and minerals into oxygen and energy-rich organic compounds. This process allows plant life to flourish on earth. In turn, animals that consume plants receive nourishment to survive, and then the animals that consume the plant eaters are ultimately affected by the sun's energy. This is known as the food chain. Another vital function of photosynthesis is the generation of oxygen that humans and animals need to survive. In return, humans and animals exhale the carbon dioxide plants need for photosynthesis. Can you visualize this segment of the earth's life cycle?

The earth's water cycle is in continuous motion, with no starting or ending point. The sun is the driving force in the water cycle. As the sun heats the water in the ocean, some of the water evaporates into the air. Also, water from plants and the soil disperses into the atmosphere. As these particles collect, cooler temperatures cause them to condense into clouds. When they become too heavy, water particles fall in the form of rain, snow, or ice. Precipitation falls to the earth because of gravity, and the cycle begins again.

Scripture Excavation

We are heading back to the book of Genesis for an exciting adventure. Read, once again, Genesis 1:1–19. What did God create on each of the first four days of creation?

_____

_____

Think through this question carefully. Plants need either direct or indirect sunlight to grow and flourish. We know that light was created on the second day and the sun was made on the fourth day. If plants require sunlight, why did God create the sun after He created the plants? Have fun with this question and add any scriptures that might support your answers.

_____

_____

Read Jeremiah 17:5–10. Break apart this block of scriptures to focus on each segment. Do comparisons with Genesis 1:1–19 to help excavate the Jeremiah verses.

Jeremiah 17:5

_____

_____

Jeremiah 17:6

_____

_____

THE SUN LINK

Jeremiah 17:7–8

Jeremiah 17:9–10

What major lesson has the Lord taught you through this analogy study?

Hidden Treasures

In your opinion, how does the sun-earth relationship correlate to your spiritual life?

Read the Reflection Pause that follows. Did God open your eyes to a new thought about His creation? What other analogies came to your mind as you read and contemplated it? Add scriptures to back up your ideas.

Celebrating Treasured Gifts

Thank God for His tender touch on your heart and soul today. Praise Him through your words as you write a praise statement.

Reflection Pause

Throughout the Bible there are numerous comparisons of the physical earth to the spiritual realm. Could it be that the Lord's creation of plants prior to His creation of the sun is symbolic of a human's need for a savior? Plants came into existence first, but for them to grow and multiply they need the sun's energy. Humans are born and exist on earth, but we are not complete until we acknowledge our sins and our need for Jesus. Once a person accepts this gift of salvation from God, Christ's light and warmth bring the soul to life. This is just like the seed of a plant that lies dormant but is brought to life when the weather conditions are right for growth to occur.

The Lord has so many incredible symbols throughout His creation! Right now, thank Him for showing you how to worship and praise Jesus, His Son, through everyday occurrences. Amen!

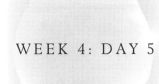

WEEK 4: DAY 5

LIGHT UP MY LIFE!

I am the light of the world. Whoever follows me will never walk in darkness, but will have the light of life.

—John 8:12

Have you experienced God's majesty? A few years ago I began thinking about this, so one day I asked the Lord to reveal His majesty to me. I basically hid this prayer in the crevices of my heart.

Later in the week, I went shopping with a friend who recently had accepted Jesus into her life. In the midst of a great time, my eyes suddenly were drawn upward to the sky. Tears welled in my eyes as I viewed a sight I had never seen or heard about before. As the sun shined brightly, a vivid rainbow encircled the sun. Each color of the rainbow glistened with radiance, intensity, and brilliance as if to sing, "Majesty, praise His glory!"

I almost fell to my knees in the parking lot, praising God. Amazement adorned my face as I shared with my friend the request I had laid before the Lord earlier that week.

God, in all His glory, chose to answer my request in a unique and personal way. As a result, not only did I have a tender moment with God's majesty, but also my new sister-in-Christ experienced God's splendor. I learned a mighty lesson that day: When you ask Him to reveal Himself to you, keep your eyes open for the way in which He chooses to make Himself known. He could use your prayer to reveal Himself to others as well. What a sweet and tender moment that I never will forget! My precious friend and I have a special "God's majesty bond" that never will be broken. Amen!

How does sunlight directly affect the human body? In Day 4, we studied the sun's effect on plants, which in turn affect humans. But direct sunlight also exercises a powerful influence on the physical and mental lives of human beings. As viewed in the diagram in Day 3, as the sun emits visible light, heat, and ultraviolet rays, the human body experiences the sun's impact. It is easy to see how visible light affects us. Ultraviolet light is unseen by the human eye and not felt by the human body, but its effects on a body's health are far-reaching.

Real Life Facts

One of the greatest health benefits of ultraviolet light is the production of vitamin D. This vitamin is essential to calcium metabolism, the formation of bone growth, and fighting skin diseases. In the northern regions of the world, the sun only shines a few hours a day throughout the winter. During this time of darkness, people are prone to depression. One reason for this disorder is a deficiency of vitamin D. Ultraviolet light has several other therapeutic effects. In some cases, it is useful in treating skin diseases, such as psoriasis and eczema. Ultraviolet light is also a key treatment for jaundice in newborn babies, which happens when a baby's liver is not fully developed and cannot rid the body of impurities.

Scripture Excavation

Our focus today is on scriptures that show how God worked behind the scenes to accomplish His will on earth. First, read John 1:1–18. Point out areas in this passage where God, through His Son, Jesus, worked behind the scenes.

_____

_____

Next, read a section of Scripture that we already excavated in Week 2: Day 2, but now examine it from a slightly different angle. Read John 9:1–5. What is Jesus' explanation of the man's birth defect? Explain how God worked in and through this situation. The Lord has sweet and tender truths to teach you. Open your heart to the powerful messages from God's Word. Praise Him for His love and mercy!

_____

_____

Are there circumstances in your life that don't make sense? Maybe you set your heart in prayer over a lifelong situation and haven't seen evidence of God at work. Could it be "this happened so that the work of God might be displayed in [your] life" (John 9:3)? How do you view your situation after studying this block of scriptures?

_____

_____

LIGHT UP MY LIFE!

The name of today's lesson is "Light Up My Life." As you read the above passage in John, what is verse 5 telling you? (For further explanation, go to Matthew 5:14–16 and John 8:12.)

_____
_____

Hidden Treasures

Remembering the facts about ultraviolet rays and the scriptures you just studied, what do you see as the correlation between them? Can you give an example of the correlation between God's Word and something occurring in your life? My prayer is that you will open your heart and share this with the group. You never know how the Lord will use it in someone else's life!

_____
_____

Celebrating Treasured Gifts

Praise God for all He has taught you this week!

_____
_____
_____
_____
_____

Reflection Pause

It is interesting that something as important to the human body as sunlight is seen with our eyes and felt on our physical bodies, yet some of its most essential health benefits go unnoticed. Isn't this like the Christian life? There are times when God allows us to view glimpses of His mighty hand of healing, peace, judgment, protection, etc. At other times, we experience the heat of situations and circumstances in life that need purification. Yet behind the scenes there are always things the Lord is doing to affect our lives. God is daily injecting doses of "spiritual vitamins" our souls need to overcome sinful diseases that work to invade our thoughts, hearts, and lives. Many times we are unaware of these expressions of God's love that are so vital to sustaining our spiritual health. Today, ask the Lord to help you grasp a new concept as you reflect on the effects sunlight has on human life.

WEEK 5

PRAYER FROM THE INSIDE OUT: THE HOLY SPIRIT INITIATES PRAYER

When you pray, go into your room, close the door and pray to your Father, who is unseen. Then your Father, who sees what is done in secret, will reward you.

—Matthew 6:6

We are moving ahead in our journey of *Reflecting Him: Living for Jesus and Loving It*! In the first part of our trek we learned that God creates a purpose for every person before conception. We are His special designs, and He desires to use us for His glory on earth. "The Pottery Process" gave us a hard and true fact to consider: life is not about me but all about Him. Amen! Next, the human sensory system analogized our physical senses of touch, aroma, taste, sight, and sound. The closer we walk with Jesus, the more sensitive we are to intimate moments with Him. Last week, we huffed and puffed our way through the study of the sun as "The Power Source" and its effects on earth. Our conclusion: life on earth would cease to exist without sunlight, just as a person would cease to exist eternally without the light of God's Son. What a blessing to know the one and only human power source, Jesus!

As we progress through this study, I want to take a moment to encourage you. The fact that you are at Week 5 is a sign of commitment. Oh, sister-friend, continue forward, seeking the Lord with all your heart. He has so many intimate things to reveal, and you don't want to miss anything. Keep it up! Allow God access to every area of your life so He can perform miracles and use you as His vessel to reach others for Christ.

We have more exciting adventures ahead that you don't want to miss! So let's go arm in arm as we travel together into "Prayer from the Inside Out."

What keeps your intimate relationship with Jesus vibrant and alive? We know that the moment we ask Jesus to be our Lord and Savior, our position in heaven is secure forever. Is that all there is to it? Absolutely not! We have the privilege of deepening the relationship with Him on a daily basis. This is like a man and woman who marry. If after the ceremony takes place the couple never takes time to have a conversation or develop their relationship, they will miss all the marriage blessings. God desires a relationship with His child that is intimate and daily connected. You may be asking yourself, *How can this be accomplished?* The number-one way is through prayer. A heart of love draws us to a place of intimacy and dependency on Jesus more than the things we do in Jesus' name. This type of prayer life will consume you with an inward focus on Him, resulting in an outward change.

This week, get ready to study "Prayer from the Inside Out." Prepare yourself for an exciting tour of the inside of your spiritual home!

Home Sweet Home

Take a moment and mentally tour every room in your home. You might start in the entryway, move to the living room, and then go to the kitchen. Now think about each bedroom. Are the beds made and all the clothes off the floor? What's under the bed, the place you might glance at every six months or so? Don't forget that out-of-the-way closet—the small, dark place you walk by daily but never enter because of what you might find inside. This week we compare your physical home to your spiritual home. Be ready to do a little renovating!

We begin with the dark, hidden room no one but you enters: the closet. Next we analyze the place designed for you to experience hours of rest: the bedroom. This is a sweet place to "be still, and know that I am God" (Ps. 46:10). From there we move to the kitchen, where we often spend many hard-working hours. In this room, we examine how the Holy Spirit moves us to labor in prayer. We then make our way into the living room to kick back and relax after a hard day's work. This is the place where we trust and have faith that He is in control! Finally, throughout the house there are windows that allow you to view your outside surroundings. How can you perceive the beauty of God's creation when the windows are smudged with dirt, water spots, and fingerprints? Get ready for a week of laughter, insight, and intimacy with God as we view the analogy of "Home Sweet Home."

WEEK 5: DAY 1

THE CLOSET

You know my folly, O God; my guilt is not hidden from you.

—Psalm 96:5

One morning as I entered the kitchen, I realized some changes had occurred during the night. Some of the leaves from my beautiful ivy plant that was located in the center of the kitchen table were missing. Upon further investigation, I found the tattered leaves strategically placed in a nest-like shape in the center of one of the chairs. I immediately thought, *Why would one of my children wake up in the middle of the night to do this?* Of course, not one of them confessed to the crime.

The next morning, to my surprise, I found the same thing. I imagined someone entering our home in the wee hours of the morning to set this weird scene. Puzzled and confused, I decided to begin breakfast. As I flung open the pantry door, something ran across the top of my feet. An electrifying shock rushed through my whole body, and my penetrating scream echoed through the house. As a result, all four children hurried to the scene. In a split second, we realized the answer regarding our mysterious villain: a rat!

Shaking profusely, I called Fred at work to share my horrible experience. Later that evening, we strategized ways to catch this home invader. He purchased one of those large rat traps—you know the ones that look like they could capture a human! We decided cheese would ensnare this intruder—at least that is what they used in the cartoons. However, the trap didn't work on this varmint! He skillfully snatched the cheese without tripping the trap.

Night after night, we tried everything from apples to peanut butter, with no luck. Finally, we resorted to plain old rat poison. One morning, to my surprise, the longest, thickest gray tail protruded out from under the utility room door. I heard the victory chant in my head: *The rat is dead! The rat is dead!* Joy and relief flooded my heart to know he met his death.

Almost a month later, while cleaning out the utility room closet, I came across the most unusual thing. In the darkest corner lay a mound of rubbish—little toys, rotten food, army men, coins, and rat evidence. The pack rat had used this dark corner to store his collectables. Guess whom he left to cleanup his mess? Yes, me.

What a life lesson! Sins we think are hidden eventually come to the surface. The pack rat, in his busyness of stealing and stashing his goods, didn't realize the death trap waiting for him. I hope you recognize the areas in your life that need to be exposed to the light so that you can experience God's mercy and grace before you get caught in a trap!

You may be wondering why we are starting this week with the closet. This is usually the place we store junk so others can't see it and we can forget about it. Remember the old saying, "Out of sight, out of mind"? Many times closets have dark corners, so their contents remain a secret unless a light shines on them. These particular closets are usually windowless and are not exposed to natural light.

It is vital that we deal with this area of our spiritual homes first. Jesus tells us to surrender it all to Him. This includes the dark things we stuff in the backs of our minds and hearts. Ask Him to reveal the hidden areas that need exposure to His Light. Experience the freedom of giving everything to the Lord as we rummage through "The Closet."

Spiritual Excavation

As we study the closets of our spiritual lives, let's narrow our focus of Scripture to David's sin with Bathsheba. Read 2 Samuel 11 and 12:1–15. Make mental notes of the progression of David's sin and how he deals with it.

In the ancient Middle East, kings went to battle during the springtime, when the weather conditions were favorable and the food supply more abundant. One of the king's responsibilities was to be with his men during battle. This allowed him to physically lead them through the war zones.

After reading this, where do you believe David's sin begins? Explain.

_____

_____

Let's do a little backtracking to examine one of the weaknesses in David's character. Read Deuteronomy 17:17. What command does God give the governing kings?

_____

_____

THE CLOSET

Read 2 Samuel 3:1–5; 5:13. What weakness did David display and what harm is caused by his actions? Also, what habit did David develop because He didn't deal with this sin? Expand on this statement, using Scripture verses to back your answers.

_____

_____

Going back to 2 Samuel 11 and 12, how did David's sin progress?

_____

_____

As David continued hiding his deeds without confessing His sins, what happened in His heart? Read 2 Samuel 11:27. What did the Lord do next? What is David's response, and what are the consequences of his actions?

_____

_____

Finally, expand on 2 Samuel 12:12. What do you learn from this verse about trying to hide sin from God and others?

_____

_____

As David continued hiding his deeds without confessing His sins, what happened in His heart? Read 2 Samuel 11:27. What did the Lord do next? How did David respond, and what consequences did he face?

_____

_____

Finally, expand on 2 Samuel 12:12. What did you learn from this verse about trying to hide sin from God and others?

_____

_____

Hidden Treasures

We can't study David's sin without looking at his prayer of repentance in Psalm 51. Think for a moment. The prophet Nathan, in 2 Samuel 12, reminds David of all the Lord had done for him. He anointed David as king over Israel and delivered him from Saul's hands. Then Nathan strategically exposed David to his own sin, almost like a floodlight illuminating the hidden, dirty corners of his heart. The words spoken out loud immediately directed David to a state of repentance. He responded with humility, not pride. Think on these aspects as you read all of Psalm 51. Which verse stands out and why?

_____

_____

Did God excuse David of all the consequences of his sin because of his repentant heart? Explain your answer using examples.

_____

_____

Celebrating Treasured Gifts

Do you feel suffocated? Has sin trapped you in the dark closets of your heart? Are you realizing a claustrophobic feeling as these walls squeeze in on you? Experience the freedom of release by repenting the transgressions in your life. Sense the presence of peace from the Holy Spirit as you unleash bitterness or anger over past hurts. God desires all of His children to be like David and acknowledge their sins, fall on their knees, <u>not give excuses</u>, and repent! Take time to pour out your heart to God through a prayer of repentance. Oh, sweet friend, let this be a life-changing moment in your walk with Jesus. Let Him free you from the closet of sin!

_____

_____

_____

_____

_____

Reflection Pause

So, why did we begin with these dark, secret, out-of-the-way places? Because it is in these closets of the heart that we tend to stuff the emotional junk that weighs heavy on the soul, such as past sins that need confessing to experience forgiveness. This is also the place where we store the wrongs done to us. If thrown in the closets of our minds and hearts, these unresolved issues spread their rot to other areas. Remember the story about the rotten potato? The same thing happens here in these hidden places of the heart. For our internal home to experience Christ's light, the closet door must be opened so that Jesus can do some house cleaning. He desires to enter every area of our spiritual homes to shine His light of love, grace, and mercy. Open up the closet so Jesus can clear the clutter!

WEEK 5: DAY 2

THE BEDROOM

Be still, and know that I am God.

—Psalm 46:10

Why is your own bed the best haven for peaceful rest? When I am out of town I often fail to get a good night's sleep. A number of things cause this discomfort, such as a hard mattress, a squeaky bed, itchy sheets, a lumpy pillow, and so on. Sometimes I lie there for hours with my eyes wide open. But the minute I get home and crawl into my own familiar bed, I have no problem falling asleep. It is in the stillness of the night that I am able to catch up on the lost sleep from the nights before. The bedroom is a place of peace, stillness, rest, and calmness!

Today I would like you to re-read Day 1's journal entry that is right after "Celebrating Treasured Gifts." What did God reveal to you? Did Jesus shine His light on a dark corner of your heart? Thank God for His revelation to you, and praise Him for His grace and mercy that are fresh every morning!

You might be asking yourself, *After my eye-opening experience yesterday, what am I supposed to do now?* From the bottom of my heart I say, "Be still and know that He is God." OK, really mull over this next question. Which part of the day are you the most still and quiet? Most people, if not all, would answer, "When I am sleeping." Of course, if you are over forty like me, uninterrupted all-night sleeps may be history. But pre-menopause and menopause is another Bible study within itself. Amen!

REFLECTING HIM

As we sleep, our bodies have the opportunity to refuel for the next day. When we deprive our bodies of needed rest, we become more vulnerable to viruses. Lack of sleep also weakens our ability to fight infections. God's design is for the human machine to refresh through these long periods of rest. Today we examine the Scriptures to see how God desires for us to spiritually rest in Him!

Scripture Excavation

Read Psalm 46. In your own words, explain why God chose to end the chapter with verses 10 and 11. Ask God to show you something special through this psalm and journal your thoughts.

_____

_____

How could you apply this psalm to your life? Break Psalm 46 into sections and give a personal anecdote to each. This might be a little challenging, but rewarding at the same time.

_____

_____

Hidden Treasures

From your own experience, give an example of a real-life situation that required you to "be still and know" that He is God. Example: praying for a child who has gone astray to come back to his relationship with Jesus.

_____

_____

This is going to be fun! Read Psalm 63:6 and rewrite this verse in your own words.

_____

_____

Have you experienced the frustration of waking up in the middle of the night and not being able to fall back to sleep? Maybe it's because God is calling you to lift your requests to Him in the stillness of the night? Possibly the Holy Spirit is prompting you to pray for someone at that very moment. Listen to His voice, and be receptive. Perhaps this time with the Lord will change you forever! Write your thoughts, adding scriptures to your answer.

_____

_____

Celebrating Treasured Gifts

It is important to realize that God is not calling you to "do" for Him but to "be" with Him. Lay your heart's requests before Jesus, and praise Him even before you know His reply. Give Him time to answer as He desires,

THE BEDROOM

so His purposes may be accomplished through you. Praise Him for the way He teaches you to "be still and know" that He is God.

_____

_____

_____

_____

_____

_____

Reflection Pause

I have to share with you an experience that I will never forget. A few years ago, I encountered some difficult circumstances as I approached the end of a time in a leadership position. Ready to throw in the towel, I contemplated terminating my commitment early. I asked the Lord for encouragement to finish the race through His strength, not mine.

The next Sunday at church, a woman stopped me in the hall. I knew of her, but didn't really know her personally. The words that came from her mouth penetrated my heart as she asked, "Are you OK? The Lord woke me up at two o'clock in the morning for three nights in a row to pray for you."

With a shock of wonder, I asked, "What were you praying?"

Her answer unlocked the closet of darkness where I hid my pain, anger, and frustration. She said, "For you to hold on! I didn't know what it meant, but I kept praying for you to hold on."

Now I want you to understand a very important point: No one knew this dilemma in my life. And I don't recall ever having a conversation with this person other than a casual "hello" while strolling through the crowd at church. No one but my husband had a clue of the thoughts filling my mind. But God, in His infinite way, called this woman in the middle of the night to stand in the gap for someone she didn't even know. Her diligence in listening to the Holy Spirit, obeying His call to pray, and then sharing the experience with me is what the Lord used to spur me forward in the last leg of the race. Oh, how thankful I am that she didn't say, "I don't have time. I don't know her. I have to get my beauty sleep!"

I learned a mighty life lesson through this experience. Now when I awake in the middle of the night, I ask the Holy Spirit for whom I can "stand in the gap" at that moment. Then as soon as I have a chance, I reveal it to the person for whom I prayed. In the bedroom, in the stillness of the night when you can't sleep, try this remedy. It works wonders! Amen!

WEEK 5: DAY 3

THE KITCHEN

Cleanse me with hyssop, and I will be clean; wash me, and I will be whiter than snow.
—Psalm 51:7

Let's examine our progress on our journey into "Prayer from the Inside Out." Praise the Lord, the closet of our minds is clean and the junk has been given to the Lord to use for His glory. The precious moments in the bedroom of our hearts taught us to "be still and know" that He is God. We realized prayer is the key to resting and trusting that God is in control of all things.

As we move forward in this examination of our souls, let's stroll into "The Kitchen." A variety of things relating to food and its preparation takes place in this room as you cut, chop, mix, bake, clean, eat, and more. It takes hard physical labor to produce a beautiful feast for the family. But the work doesn't stop at the dinner table. Clean up always has to follow. If dirty dishes sit for a long period, the cleaning is more difficult. As a result, it is in the best interest of all concerned to use the clean-as-you-go technique so that the kitchen is fresh and attractive whenever friends stop in.

Just as laboring in the kitchen represents an expression of physical love, prayer suggests a labor of spiritual love. Today we compare the character of the kitchen to the character qualities of a person dedicated to prayer. We focus on the Holy Spirit and His encouragement to pray specifically. This loving labor of prayer draws us to a more intimate relationship with Jesus.

Scripture Excavation

Do you ever find yourself walking into the kitchen not knowing what to fix for supper? It happens to me all the time. I start rummaging through the pantry and refrigerator to figure out what I can create at the last minute. This is like our prayer life in many ways. Sometimes we begin praying and our thoughts are so muddled that we fumble around, trying to decide exactly what to pray. Many times we simply say a quick surface prayer. It is like grabbing a "Dinner in the Box," ready to eat in five minutes. You have no idea what is in the box, but you know something will come out. God desires our prayers to be thorough, as if we were helping to prepare a feast. You know, the kind of meal that requires cutting, chopping, measuring, stirring, heating, cleaning, etc. When we seek the Lord with all of our hearts, He will guide us in how to pray. When we labor in prayer, it requires our time, energy, devotion, stillness, love, selflessness, and listening skills. We don't want to miss the prayer feast God has prepared for us to enjoy!

Study Romans 8:26–39. What does this block of Scripture tell us about the Holy Spirit's role when we pray? Why does this create tenderness in our hearts?

_____

_____

Read John 16:5–15. The subtitle to this block of Scripture is "The Work of the Holy Spirit." Why did Jesus tell His disciples it is for their good that He goes away? Explain your thoughts in detail.

_____

_____

In regard to prayer, the Holy Spirit is titled the "Counselor." What does this mean?

_____

_____

Now that you have studied these passages of Scripture and answered some questions, let's have a little fun. Make an analogy of your own regarding the kitchen and the Holy Spirit. Ask the Lord to open your heart so that you hear from Him as you write your thoughts. I wish I could read your answers!

_____

_____

Hidden Treasures

Now let's turn our attention to an example of struggling through prayer. Read Luke 22:39–46. Before Jesus' arrest, He went to the Garden of Gethsemane to pray. He needed to spend time with His Father before His arrest, trial, and death on the cross. Give examples of Jesus' laboring through prayer.

_____

_____

THE KITCHEN

Why does God call us to toil in prayer for others as well as for ourselves? Do you always know when a trial is going to consume your life? Ask God to reveal some mighty things through this question!

_____

_____

_____

_____

Celebrating Treasured Gifts

Let's practice! Take time to create a "prayer feast," asking the Holy Spirit to be your Master Chef. Ask Him to guide you through the recipe as you add all the necessary ingredients. Listen to His prompting as you pour your prayer items into the bowl. Then mix for the appropriate amount of time. Of course, most recipes call for some heat for the cuisine to turn out perfectly. God has a special banquet waiting after you labor in prayer!

_____

_____

_____

_____

_____

_____

Reflection Pause

Have you ever made stew? The recipe calls for cutting and chopping meat, carrots, potatoes, celery, cabbage, mushrooms, tomatoes, onions, garlic, green beans, and more. The amount of salt and spices is very important for the flavor to be just right. If you tasted the mixture right after all the ingredients were dumped in the pot, you probably would not come back for more. The ingredients need time to simmer and blend together to create a delicious flavor. It is the same with prayer. The more we stir the "prayer pot," the more God blends the prayers to form a savory mixture that keeps people coming back for more. Keep laboring in prayer as the Holy Spirit leads. Amen!

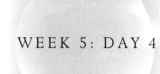

WEEK 5: DAY 4

THE LIVING ROOM

For the glory of the Lord filled his temple.

—1 Kings 8:11

After laboring in "The Kitchen," we are moving into the warmth of "The Living Room." This is the place to rest and kick off our shoes after a long day's work, leaving behind our day-to-day responsibilities. It is in this room where we discuss the day's events with others, sit by the fire, read a book, play games, reminisce about the past, and more. In the living room, everyone has his own favorite place to snuggle. So get cozy as you relax in your spiritual living room and learn to trust, have faith, and praise God that He is in control.

Spiritual Excavation

Today we are going to do a little Old Testament excavating. Read 1 Kings 8:1–21. Make note of specific events that occurred as they brought the Ark into the temple.

_____

_____

In your own words, explain 1 Kings 8:10–12. What does the cloud symbolize? Use other scriptures to back up your analogy, including those we studied this week.

_____

_____

What is significant about 1 Kings 8:14–21, focusing on verse 14? What does Solomon do first after the Ark is secure? How can you apply this verse to your life?

_____

_____

At the end of 1 Kings 8:2 is a reference to a feast in the seventh month. Tracing events of this time of year, we find this is actually the Feast of Tabernacles. This feast takes place at the conclusion of the ceremonial year, honoring God for granting rest in the Promised Land for His people (see Lev. 23:33–44). This feast celebrated the harvest and was a time of thanksgiving for God's protection of the Israelites. How appropriate for this celebration to occur after the completion of the temple and after the Ark of the Covenant had been carried into the Most Holy Place. It is important to note that the Ark, which held the Ten Commandants written on two stone tablets, a jar of manna, and Aaron's budded rod, symbolized God's presence in the midst of His people.

Hidden Treasures

Read Solomon's prayer of dedication in 1 Kings 8:22–53. What stands out in this scripture?

_____

_____

Read 1 Kings 8:54–61. What is in Solomon's heart as he blesses the assembly?

_____

_____

How can you apply these same characteristics to your own life?

_____

_____

_____

_____

Celebrating Treasured Gifts

Remember that you are in the living room of your spiritual home. You recently labored with a heart of prayer in the kitchen. Now it is time to rest, trust, and have faith that God has heard your prayers. As you remember

THE LIVING ROOM

these analogies, what other thoughts come to mind? Maybe you need to praise Him, like Solomon. Have fun, and see that the Lord has something sweet today!

_____

_____

_____

_____

_____

_____

Reflection Pause

I cannot go another day without sharing a special moment between the Lord and me. While writing Day 1 of "Prayer from the Inside Out," I prayed, "Lord, I don't know how I am going to afford to get this Bible study published. Lack of funds is a big problem, but I trust You to handle this dilemma. If You provide the funds, I am going to praise You; and if the study doesn't get published, I am going to praise You. No matter what the outcome, our time together working on this project has been wonderful! Amen!"

Two days later, I received a phone call. A dear friend, whom I have known for more than twenty years, said her husband wanted to visit with me.

In our conversation, he shared how his corporation is dedicated to furthering God's kingdom. As a result, they pray for ministries their company can support. Then he continued, "After taking a look at the heart of Reflective Life Ministries, we would like to support your ministry in the amount of _____."

His actions followed the verse: "to him who is able to do immeasurably more than all we ask or imagine" (Eph. 3:20–21). Shock filled my mind and body! All I could think about was my prayer forty-eight hours prior to this conversation and how I had said, "Lord, this Bible study is Yours. I trust You to do what You want with it."

He then said to me, "How big do you think God is, Carla? Open the door, and let God go beyond what your mind can conceive. Continue to do all He is calling you to do for His kingdom. Encourage women to live their lives sold out to Jesus. Use your God-given talents for His glory!"

I cried for two days! It is not the amount of money that matters. It is God providing. God used this on-the-spot training to teach me to pray and let go so that God can do His work. I pray this encourages you as you pray for situations in your life. Don't miss a moment when the Holy Spirit is prompting you to pray. He has some on-the-spot training for you as well!

WEEK 5: DAY 5

THE WINDOWS

About midnight Paul and Silas were praying and singing hymns to God, and the other prisoners were listening to them.

—Acts 16:25

This week we have gone through the inside of our spiritual homes, doing some major house cleaning. Do you notice freshness in the air? By giving Jesus access to the closets in our lives, His light exposed the hidden areas that needed cleaning. "The Bedroom" allowed us to see the need to "be still and know" that He is God. This prepared the way for the chores to be done in "The Kitchen." After a hard day's work, we put up our feet in "The Living Room," trusting God is in control. But is this all there is to living a life sold out to Jesus?

Let's look at a different scenario. You have come to the point of realizing that God is in control of everything. As you sit in your living room, your eyes move to a window. The view is spectacular! The scene looks like a picture postcard. The rolling hills have a fresh, new blanket of green grass. The birds are flittering back and forth, as if playing a game of tag. Suddenly, your view becomes distorted as your focus narrows and you notice water spots on the window. Then you detect a faint film of dirt built up during the winter months. Oh, my, what about all those fingerprints? The beauty beyond the window is obstructed by the blemishes on the window itself.

Isn't this like life? We give Jesus access to cleansing our souls, but for some reason we easily become sidetracked with our daily activities. We find ourselves having trouble looking beyond the distractions. Instead of looking for God in the midst of a situation, we find ourselves focusing on the actual circumstances. We need to get out our window cleaner and shine the glass so that we have a clear picture of what lies beyond the window. Ask the Lord to prepare your heart to hear from Him today as you study "The Windows" of the soul.

Scripture Excavation

How do you find joy in the midst of your trials? It goes beyond putting a smile on your face and living behind a mask. Today we focus our study on a couple of men who didn't base their joy on their circumstances, but instead on their relationship with Jesus.

Read Acts 16:16–34. In your own words, explain the scene taking place. One thing to note: in Acts 16:1, Paul and Silas were on their way to the church to pray. Why is this important?

_____

_____

Was this imprisonment justified or unjustified? In other words, what had they done to deserve being thrown in prison?

_____

_____

How did they handle this horrible predicament that God allowed to happen to them? What attitudes did Paul and Silas portray while in prison? Include scriptures to back up your answers.

_____

_____

Who watched Paul and Silas from within the jail? How did God use Paul and Silas to bring glory to Himself?

_____

_____

What part did prayer play in this block of verses? What were the results of God's answer to these prayers?

_____

_____

Hidden Treasures

Is God using a situation in your life to allow you an opportunity to praise Him? If so, write it down and compare your attitude to that of Paul and Silas. Are there any changes you need to make? Is God calling you to trust and have faith that He is in control?

_____

_____

What are some practical ways in which you can respond to the mishaps in life? Review Acts 16 for some examples. Add other scriptures to your answer so you can share them with your group. What a wonderful way to grow and learn from one another!

_____

_____

Celebrating Treasured Gifts

Breathe in the Holy Spirit's freshness as He shows you how to pray. Pour out your heart in praise to God for all He is teaching you. Express your love to Him through a prayer, poem, song, analogy, or in whatever way you are led.

You're doing a great job! Keep it up, sister. We are halfway through the study. You don't want to miss the hidden treasures waiting for you in the rest of the study!

_____

_____

_____

_____

_____

Reflection Pause

Reflect for a moment on a couple of important points. First, notice how this whole situation began. In verse 16, Paul and Silas were on their way to pray when a girl met them who was indwelt by an evil spirit. This is relevant to believers because we need to recognize that the enemy is waiting to attack us before we pray. He wants to halt anything that the Lord is doing to further the development of God's kingdom. We must prepare ourselves by consistently praying and worshipping the Lord, seeking Jesus daily, and loving others. Be aware, the enemy is waiting to attack when you least expect it.

The second point of reference is in verse 25. Here we see that Paul and Silas's joy was not based on their circumstances. They weren't singing a "pity me, I am in jail" song. No, in the darkest part of the night they were praying and singing praises to God, and the prisoners were listening. Wow, what witnesses they were for Jesus! Because they were willing vessels with the right attitudes, God used their undeserved circumstances to bring others to Jesus. Praise God for the way He weaves His miracles in your life so that others may witness a life sold out to Jesus!

WEEK 6

PRAYER FUELS FAITH: PRAYER ENERGIZES FAITH INTO ACTION

Now faith is being sure of what we hope for and certain of what we do not see.
—Hebrews 11:1

*F*aith. Do you find yourself struggling in this area of your Christian life? What is faith? What does it mean to be "sure of what we hope for and certain of what we do not see"?

Do you fear falling asleep because you might stop breathing? No, by faith you lie down in your bed, close your eyes, and before you know it, you're fast asleep. Your body is not only breathing the oxygen it needs but also is physically rejuvenating itself for the next day.

When a baby is learning to walk, he or she doesn't stop trying after the first tumble to the ground. Without thinking, he or she gets up and starts all over again. It's actually a bit comical. Yet the baby has no idea he or she trusts his or her parents to catch him or her when he or she falls. That's total faith without a worry in the world!

You might be asking yourself, *What does prayer have to do with faith?* This week we will uncover the way "Prayer Fuels Faith"!

Gasoline Supply Chain

How often do you put gasoline in your vehicle? The older you get, the more it becomes just another routine procedure. Visualize yourself pumping gas into your car, turning the key, and igniting the engine. Now ask yourself how gasoline becomes the energy that makes your car go.

This week we track the gasoline supply chain, beginning with the exploration for oil that determines the drilling location. Next it is very important to prepare the equipment properly for the drilling process. Then we examine the extraction, followed by refining the petroleum product. Finally, the gas pump delivers the fuel to the consumer. Our tour guide for the week is Fred McDougal—yes, my man! He is a petroleum engineer and has worked in the industry for more than twenty-five years. His expert technical skills make him a perfect tour guide as we study the different aspects of the gasoline supply chain.

I am praying that you will learn something new this week about placing your faith in God. Have fun as you venture through "Prayer Fuels Faith"!

Prayers
Cara Lee
Wendy
Chris' job situation

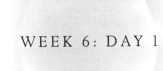

WEEK 6: DAY 1

TRUSTING THE UNSEEN

Now faith is being sure of what we hope for and certain of what we do not see.
—Hebrews 11:1

"Surely she is not old enough to drive! Not the baby of the family!" These words poured from my mouth as our youngest child passed her driver's permit test. I have to admit that I wasn't ready for her to be at that stage in life. Not that I doubted her ability to be a great driver, but this was another step closer to her independence from Dad and Mom.

As she proudly buckled herself behind the wheel, a sudden fear jumped into my thoughts. You know, the old "what ifs" that invade your mind like a swarm of bees. *What if she doesn't see a car coming toward her? What if she doesn't stop in time at a red light? What if she freezes while driving?* After I caught my breath, the Lord reminded me that He is in control. My job is to teach her to be a responsible driver, pray for her safety, and trust Him.

Are you sure about trusting the unseen? How can you put your trust in something without seeing tangible evidence? Faith means being confident of God's authenticity, even though you are not sure of the outcome or of what the future holds. Faith is not just a belief in God, but truly believing God. Belief in God is necessary for a relationship with Him through His Son, Jesus. But if you stop there, you miss the other blessings God has waiting for you.

Do you believe that God is true to His Word? Do you believe that God means what He says? Whether you see evidence or not, do you still trust Him to follow through with His promises? Ask the Lord to open your heart as we study "Trusting the Unseen."

Real Life Facts

Today we examine the first step in the gasoline supply chain: exploration. It's easy to take things for granted, and fuel is no exception. Most people do not understand the process behind the development of the gasoline they put into their tanks. Where does this fuel originate? To answer this question, we must go back many years. Oil is formed by the remains of tiny plants and animals that died in ancient seas. These organisms sank to the bottom of the ocean floor and over time became trapped under layers of sediment. Because there was no oxygen to destroy the plant and animal materials, the temperature and pressure within the buried layers increased as more layers accumulated. Eventually the raw organic material distilled into what is known as crude oil.

How do the experts locate this crude oil? Exploration starts with choosing a location and developing a plan. The explorer must describe how his prospect meets all the necessary conditions so he can sell it to his management or investors. Surface geology and geochemical, magnetic, and seismic data are available to justify the prospect. In all honesty, it requires faith! Faith in the data, the plan, the source, and what they speculate but can't see. Faith!

Scripture Excavation

This week we study the lives of a few Heroes of Faith. Each day we review Hebrews 11 and then dive into other scriptures to discover why God gave this hero a "Faith Badge." There is no better place to begin than with a man who loved God with all his heart. God called him to act "Trusting the Unseen." He is none other than Noah! Read Hebrews 11:7. From this verse what do you learn about Noah?

_____

_____

Why Noah? Read Genesis 6:1–12. Explain what was happening at the time and why God chose Noah.

_____

_____

Read Genesis 6:13–22. Where do you see Noah "Trusting the Unseen"?

_____

_____

Hidden Treasures

Let your mind do a little wondering and imagine yourself as Noah's wife. As your husband begins building this giant "thing" out of wood, you notice the neighbors whispering to one another. The gossip travels so fast through town that you are now faced with a choice: trust your husband's faith in God or, like the others, believe he has gone off the deep end. Add your own thoughts to this scenario, and don't forget that Noah is the spiritual leader of your family. Have fun with this assignment!

_____

_____

In light of what you wrote above, read Genesis 7 and 8. As Noah's wife, what are you thinking now?

_____

_____

Before the great Flood, had the earth ever experienced rain? This question has been a source of debate for centuries. Scholars and scientists have discussed the facts from every angle and still aren't sure of the answer. Genesis 2:5–6 says, "No shrub of the field had yet appeared on the earth and no plant of the field had yet sprung up, for the Lord God had not sent rain on the earth . . . but streams came up from the earth and watered the whole surface of the ground." If you didn't put these words in context with other scriptures, you might conclude that water didn't fall from the sky before the flood. Yet after reading other verses, you might conclude that this part of creation was a work in progress.

Regardless, we know that there had never been an actual flood before this time. Reading the first part of Genesis 6, we learn God's disappointment in man was so great that He was sorry He had even made man—to the point that He grieved in His heart! Can you feel His frustration and disappointment? Think back on the forgiveness He poured out on Adam. By Noah's time, all mankind had disappointed Him—except for Noah. Genesis 6:8 (NKJV) says, "But Noah found grace in the eyes of the Lord." Whether there was rain before God confronted Noah is of no importance. The significant idea is that Noah had faith in God even when things didn't make sense to him. Genesis 6:22 is proof of Noah's faith: "Noah did . . . according to all that God commanded him."

Celebrating Treasured Gifts

Are you facing a situation in your life where God is calling you to have faith in Him regardless of the circumstances? Think of Noah's situation. Notice how in Genesis 6 he said "yes" to God without questioning Him. He followed all of God's commands without complaining. Write a prayer to God about your situation and your desire to have total faith like Noah. This "exploration" step requires faith: in the data, the plan, the source, and what you speculate but can't see!

_____

_____

Reflection Pause

Remember the story of my daughter getting her driver's permit? Recall the thoughts that poured into my head. Isn't this a lot like life? As we drive through our daily lives we are struck with thoughts that sideswipe our trust and faith in God—things like when a mammogram comes back inconclusive and you require additional tests. All of a sudden, the "what ifs" start flooding in from every direction. Fear begins to replace the trust God calls us to have in Him.

Oh, sweet friend, pray that when these times come into your life you will replace fear with trust. Exchange the "what ifs" with "Trusting the Unseen"!

WEEK 6: DAY 2

PREPARING THE HEART

Without faith it is impossible to please God, because anyone who comes to him must believe that he exists and that he rewards those who earnestly seek Him.

—Hebrews 11:6

"Without faith it is impossible to please God." Really think about those words for a moment. This is a very strong statement the writer of Hebrews made.

How does faith grow? Is faith inevitable, or does it take time to develop faith in God? Today we look at these questions and more as we study "Preparing the Heart."

Did you wake up with thoughts of Jesus on your heart, mind, and soul? He is waiting every morning for our first thoughts to be about Him—to praise Him for who He is, what He has done, and how He works all things to His glory.

So often when the alarm rings we hit the snooze button a few times, which leads to the "Late Again" disorder. We fly out of bed and then rush, rush, rush to get ready for the day so we're not late for our appointments, church, work, school, etc. All the while, Jesus is on the back burner of our minds. In His tenderness, He never pushes Himself on us. He desires for His children to seek Him, search the Word, worship Him, and call upon the name of the Lord in all things.

When my children were younger, they knew I loved to spend quiet time with the Lord in the morning. They observed this on a regular basis (hint, hint: I said "regular," not *all* the time!). Anyway, one day after dealing with the kids arguing and fussing, I finally hit the point of blast-off. I sent all four children to different parts of the house to bring some calmness back into our home. From one room I heard Luke, eight years old at the time, ask a question that penetrated my heart. In fact, it still lingers in the crevices of my mind. He said, "Mama, I need to ask you an important question. Did you have your quiet time with the Lord this morning?" All of a sudden, I realized I had not even thought about the Lord that day. Before getting out of bed my wheels had been spinning ninety miles an hour, planning the tasks for the day. No thought of Jesus had entered my heart, soul, or mind.

How can my faith grow in the Lord if I don't take time to be with Him? Oh, what we can learn from the mouths of babes!

Real Life Facts

The second step in the gasoline supply chain is the drilling process. The only way to definitively determine whether or not crude oil is available in commercial quantities is to drill an actual hole in the reservoir. This is usually done after sufficient acreage has been acquired around a viable prospect. A drill site is cleared and leveled, and access roads are built. Water is a necessity to the drilling process, so if there is not a natural source of water, the company has to drill a water well. Also, there is a need for a reserve pit, which is used to hold and sometimes dispose of drilling mud and rock cuttings during the drilling process. It is usually lined with plastic to protect the environment. If the drilling site is in an ecologically sensitive area or is federally protected, the cuttings and mud must be trucked off-site.

The crew then sets up the rig and drills a surface hole to a pre-set depth. This drilling requires placing the bit on heavyweight pipe known as a "drill collar" and "drill pipe." As the drill pipe is rotated and weight is applied to the bit, mud circulates through the pipe and out of the bit to lift rock cuttings out of the hole. As the hole gets deeper, additional drill pipe is added. After reaching the pre-set depth, a larger string of pipe known as "casing" is cemented in the freshly-drilled hole. This prevents the hole from collapsing and provides a means of controlling the well when oil and gas zones are penetrated. Centralizers are placed around the outside of the casing pipe to keep it centered in the hole. Additional casing sections are added until the oil zone is penetrated. Now the hole is ready for testing to see if crude oil is there for the taking. What an expensive, yet crucial, process! The whole time the drilling company and rig hands move forward in the drilling process, they trust crude oil will be found. If they only speculated where the oil might be but did not actually drill, discoveries never would be made.

The same is true in our Christian lives. As we put our trust in the Lord, we move ahead in the calling He has for our lives. The "Hero of Faith" we study today experienced much trusting and pressing forward. God promised him something that didn't come to pass for years, but he kept the faith. Who is this Hero of Faith? Abraham!

PREPARING THE HEART

Scripture Excavation

"By faith Abraham, when called to go to a place he would later receive as his inheritance, obeyed and went, even though he did not know where he was going. By faith he made his home in the Promised Land like a stranger in a foreign country" (Heb. 11:8–9).

Keep in mind the name of today's study: "Preparing the Heart." Read Hebrews 11:8–19. Point out some verses where you see Abraham preparing for the fulfillment of God's promises.

_____

_____

We need to take a trip into the Old Testament to learn more about Abraham's life. When we first meet this Hero of Faith, his name is "Abram," which means "exalted father." As his relationship with God developed, God changed his name to "Abraham," meaning "father of many." Read Genesis 12:1–9. What do you learn about this man? How old was he?

_____

_____

Now read Genesis 15. What did God see in Abram and what was His promise to him?

_____

_____

Throughout Genesis we observe Abram's faith in God. Read Genesis 17:1–8 and 17. What did God say when He appeared this time? How old were Abraham and Sarah now?

_____

_____

Abraham's faith was not based on what he saw God do but on God Himself. He trusted God in every way. If God said it, He meant it. Oh, what faith! How many years did Abraham wait for God to fulfill His promise?

_____

_____

Read Genesis 21:1–7. Explain in your own words Abraham's reaction to Sarah's pregnancy, the birth, and the circumcision. How did Sarah react, and what did she expect from others?

_____

_____

REFLECTING HIM

Hidden Treasures

In your opinion, why did God wait so long to fulfill the promise? Really pray and think through this question.

Genesis 20:17 (NKJV) says, "So Abraham prayed to God; and God healed Abimelech, his wife, and his female servants. Then they bore children." Read the next few verses, Genesis 21:1–7. What happened?

Celebrating Treasured Gifts

This prayer represented Abraham's first time to initiate a prayer to God. Could God have been waiting for Abraham to come to Him in prayer before He fulfilled His promise? Think about it: If prayer energizes faith into action, did God want Abraham to understand the power of prayer? How can you apply this to your own life? I wish I could read your answer!

Reflection Pause

You have accomplished some major Scripture excavation today. Reading about Abraham's trust in God is so encouraging! Don't forget the name of this week's study: "Prayer Fuels Faith." Here is a storyboard showing Abraham's trust in God:

Genesis 12:1–3—The Lord said to Abram (age seventy-five); Abram did as the Lord commanded (vv. 4–6).
Genesis 12:7—The Lord appeared to Abram; he moved on as the Lord commanded (v. 9).
Genesis 13:14—The Lord said to Abram; he moved his tent as the Lord commanded (v. 18).
Genesis 15:1—The Lord came to Abram in a vision; he believed (v. 6).
Genesis 17:1—The Lord appeared to Abram (age ninety-nine); Abram fell on his face before God (v. 3).
Genesis 18:1—The Lord appeared to Abraham; he did as the Lord commanded (vv. 6–8).

PREPARING THE HEART

Notice all of the times that the Lord reached out to Abraham. We see Abraham always willing to listen and obey. Abraham waited twenty-five years for the son the Lord had promised him. Throughout those long years, Abraham trusted God to follow through with His promise of Genesis 17:16 (NKJV), "I will bless her [Sarah] and also give you a son by her; then I will bless her, and she shall be a mother of nations, kings of peoples shall be from her." Trust Him today with your prayers. God's timing is always perfect and never too late. Amen!

WEEK 6: DAY 3

DIGGIN' IN!

What does it profit, my brethren, if someone says he has faith but does not have works?
—James 2:14 NKJV

Diggin' In—this sounds difficult, labor intensive, and time-consuming. But for faith to mature, there must be some burrowing into God's Word before you can apply the concepts to your life. "Faith" in the Greek is *pistis*, which essentially means the belief that God exists. He is the Creator and Ruler of all things. Through Jesus Christ, God gives all humanity the opportunity for eternal salvation. Today, have fun "Diggin' In" and discovering new territories of faith.

Real Life Facts

Step three in the gasoline supply chain is the extraction process. Once a discovery is made, the accumulation of materials is evaluated to determine if it is commercially viable to further develop the well. Estimates of the volume of oil in the accumulation, the rate at which the reservoir will deliver oil to the hole, and the cost to drill the well must also be evaluated. These educated guesses along with predictions of future oil prices and tax rates are assessed in the economics of developing the discovery.

If the project is determined to be feasible, the rig is removed and a pump jack is placed over the well. If the well doesn't flow on its own, a pump jack is added to lift the oil to the surface. This motor's rotational energy is converted to an up and down motion by means of the pump jack's arms and beam. On the up stroke, oil is pulled into a pump barrel. On the down stroke, oil is discharged from the pump into the tubing string. The pump jack's up and down motion continually lifts oil to the surface.

Wow, does this sound like digging into the Word and spending time with God? When we are consistent in reading the Bible, it is like the continuous motion of a pump jack. When we read the Word—searching, meditating, and applying—it's similar to striking oil! But if we never take the time to read God's Word, like a pump jack ceasing to move, we forfeit the opportunity to develop a deeper walk with Jesus. So without delay, let's begin "Diggin' In"!

Scripture Excavation

Can you think of a great Hero of Faith who put his total trust in God when he led the Israelites out of Egypt? You probably already guessed: Moses.

Moses left behind a spiritual legacy that encourages believers in their journey with God. Read Acts 7:17–35 along with Hebrews 11:23–29. After reading these two passages, what jumps out at you about Moses?

_____

_____

Let's backtrack to the Old Testament for a deeper understanding of Moses' life. Because this isn't an exhaustive study on Moses, we will focus on just one aspect: the beginning of his life. Read Exodus 1 to set the stage and then 2:1–10. Explain in your own words what the Israelites were facing.

_____

_____

How did God work behind the scenes in the midst of the Israelites' turmoil?

_____

_____

Speculate on the relationship Moses' mom had with God. In Exodus 2:1–10, where do you see her faith displayed, and did she receive any blessings?

_____

_____

Can you imagine placing your three-month-old baby in a homemade basket in the reeds by a riverbank? What thoughts must have rushed through Moses' mother's mind? The basket could have leaked, snakes could have crawled in, and bugs could have bitten the baby. Put yourself in her place:

_____

_____

DIGGIN' IN!

Hidden Treasures

The summary of Moses' life in Acts 7 and Hebrews 11 proves that God considered Moses a man of great faith. Moses didn't want a shallow relationship with God. He dug in deep with his whole body, mind, and soul. But what created this desire within him? Could it have been something to do with his mother's faith in the only true God, her heart for prayer, and her steadfast trust in God while she watched her son grow up in Pharaoh's palace?

_____

_____

Let's look at another man with tremendous faith. Read 2 Timothy 1:5. How did Timothy's mother and grandmother influence his life?

_____

_____

Keeping Timothy's example in mind, what impact did Moses' mother have on Moses and her other children? When did his mother's influence and prayers make a difference? List specific examples and scriptures you discover. Make this a fun research question, and allow the Holy Spirit to teach you something fresh and new.

_____

_____

Celebrating Treasured Gifts

Here is where the rubber meets the road. Write an analogy between Moses' faith and the extraction process from Real Life Facts. Journal your thoughts, and praise the Lord for the way He uses real life events to teach His truths!

May today's lesson encourage you to live your life daily by "Diggin' In" to God's Word!

_____

_____

Reflection Pause

More than likely you have fallen into this cycle at one time or another: wake up in the morning, immediately hit the ground running, crawl into bed at night, and while falling asleep finally say the words, "Dear God . . ." We become so intoxicated with our own issues and circumstances that one day bleeds into the next to the point that we live to exist. This is not God's plan for us! He desires for us to live a life sold out to Jesus. From the moment we awake, He is waiting for us to connect with Him in prayer. God desires to spend quality time with us. But He will never push Himself on us. He has a daily agenda for each of His children. It is up to us to receive the assignment for the day!

WEEK 6: DAY 4

MOVE INTO ACTION!

What does it profit, my brethren, if someone says he has faith but does not have works?
—James 2:14 NKJV

Mission trips deepen your faith in wonderful ways. A few years ago I experienced the blessings of such a trip. Many people in the impoverished community we visited were unaware of the gift of God's salvation and Jesus' grace. Every evening we set up a crusade area in the streets. The local men built a stage, which resulted in a "faith" issue every night because of the materials they used. As our people readied themselves for the crusade each evening, I wondered, *Will the stage hold all the sound equipment, musical instruments, band members, and the preacher? Oh, Lord, please direct your angels to bring stability to this dilapidated structure called a stage!*

The electricity to the stage created another area of trust. Imagine an unrolled, tangled skein of yarn—that is what the electrical lines resembled. They connected in every direction, with no order whatsoever. Each evening the locals pirated the electricity from a line somewhere above the stage. As a "woman of caution," I prayed mightily for the connections each evening.

On the last day of the mission trip, rain poured all day. The question arose as to whether or not we should attempt the last crusade, but after much prayer, we felt the Lord leading us to do it. With the stage erected and the electricity bootlegged, the final service commenced. As the praise band led worship, a joyful noise filled the air for miles around. All of a sudden, a clap of thunder escaped the heavens, and a bolt of lightning flashed across the sky. Electricity sparks shot off in all directions. Fear permeated my whole body as I watched my two oldest boys on that wobbly stage surrounded by unstable wiring. I closed my eyes and cried, *Please, God, stop the rain! Please calm the storm that is brewing. These people need to hear about Jesus, and my boys need Your safe hand of protection!* When I opened my eyes, I couldn't believe it. The clouds parted, and the moon shined through as if God were singing, "Alleluia." Come to find out, almost the whole mission team prayed the same thing at exactly the same time. At that moment, my faith in God jumped to a whole new level. Prayer absolutely fuels faith into action. Look for opportunities to deepen your faith this week. They are all around you!

Is faith active or passive? This is a great reflective question! When someone has faith in Jesus, he is choosing to accept Jesus as the Way, the Truth, and the Life. The person acknowledging this faith actively accepts this criterion to be true. But a number of steps are required for that faith to "Move into Action." Today we will study a few building blocks of faith.

Real Life Facts

Step four in the gasoline supply chain is known as the refining process. Perhaps you have seen movies such as *The Beverly Hillbillies* or *Giant,* where they strike oil and it comes gushing out of the ground. As shown on the big screen, crude oil in its raw form is a thick, black substance. But that isn't what it looks like when you pump gasoline into your car. By that time, it is almost clear. How can you start with crude oil and end with gasoline? How does crude oil become the key ingredient to other products, such as kerosene, plastic, heating oil, tires, synthetic fibers, and crayons? What makes it possible for the same source to create so many products? The process is known as refining.

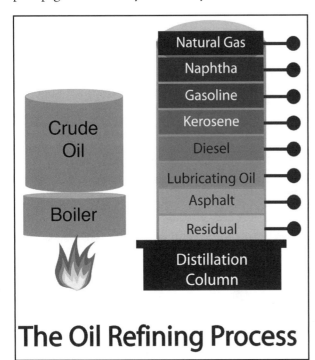

Crude oil contains all sorts of hydrocarbons. The oil refining process separates everything into useful substances or fractions. The oldest and most common way to separate these fractions is the boiling point method. Basically, crude oil is heated until it condenses into different vapors, separated in the distillation column according to their density. The different levels are then extracted and used to produce fuel, chemicals, and other products.

Scripture Excavation

Today's Hero of Faith illustrates this week's life connection. God called this man to lead the Israelite army against the Midianites, who were destroying the Israelites' homes and fields. Although doubtful and fearful, Gideon said "yes" to God. Gideon knew his own weaknesses, as well as the Israelite army's insufficiencies. But despite these inadequacies, he allowed the Lord to use him.

Read Hebrews 11:32–34. What other Heroes of Faith are listed with Gideon? Of what significance is this list?
Barak, Samson, Jephthah, David, Samuel - together their faith-justice & strength made them powerful

MOVE INTO ACTION!

Explain what the Israelites were experiencing at this time. What did God do for His people, and how did they respond? (See Judges 6:1–10.)

hard times - abandonment -

What happened next? (See Judges 6:11–24.)

Read the rest of Judges 6:24–40 and Judges 7 to really understand the way Gideon obeyed God despite his doubts and fears. Where do you see God encouraging Gideon in these passages? How does this encourage you?

Hidden Treasures

How else can you compare our spiritual lives to the oil refining process? Have fun sharing these correlations with your group.

Celebrating Treasured Gifts

What have you learned today, and how has your faith been encouraged through studying our Hero of Faith, Gideon? Write your heartfelt prayer and praise to the Lord.

Reflection Pause

How does Gideon's relationship with God compare to the oil refining process? After God gave him an assignment, Gideon continually sought God's direction and guidance as he moved forward. Gideon didn't rely on his own strength to accomplish God's assigned tasks. Look back at the oil refining diagram. Think of Gideon as the crude oil tank and God as the boiler. In this comparison, the distillation column or the end result occurs because of communication with the Lord. He takes all our impurities and breaks them apart to make them useful to God's kingdom. God filters our fears and doubts just like the boiler distills the petroleum products. This spiritual refining process is a wonderful example of "when we are weak He is strong"!

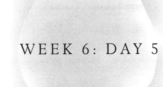

WEEK 6: DAY 5

THE OUTCOME

These were all commended for their faith, yet none of them received what had been promised.
—Hebrews 11:39

Have you ever had one of those days? You know, the kind you would rather forget?

With my friend's permission, I will share one of his "A Day in My Life" stories. The beginning of this particular day started with work deadlines, sick children, and an argument with his wife. These problems caused him to run behind schedule, which affected his departure for an out-of-town funeral. As he jumped into his truck, he realized that his gas gauge registered empty. So he stopped at a convenience store, swiped his credit card, put the gas nozzle into the gas tank, and pulled the trigger on the nozzle. While waiting in the truck for his tank to fill up, he replayed the day's events over and over in his head.

On the road again and trying to make up for lost time, he headed towards his destination. Before long, he noticed people in other vehicles pointing and giving him odd hand signals. At first he ignored them, but then it began to annoy him as the gestures continued. He finally pulled off the road to see what they were pointing to on his truck. To his astonishment, the gas pump nozzle was sticking out from his tank with the gas hose trailing behind his pickup's tailgate! Because of his concern over the day's events and his time crunch, he forgot to put the nozzle back on the pump and replace the gas cap. What to do next? He bounced his options back and forth—*Return the hose to the store or trek on down the road to the funeral?*

After debating with the Lord, he turned the truck around and made his way back to the store. When he pulled the broken hose out of the truck bed and handed it to the store clerk, she said with shock in her voice, "Most people don't bring it back!" He let out a sigh of relief, knowing he did the right thing. What's funny is this is not the first time but the second time that this happened to my friend. I laughed so hard at his misadventure!

What a great real life story to end "Prayer Fuels Faith." After we allow the Lord to fill us with what we need for the day, it is important to stay focused on Him. If not, we could end up like my friend, focusing attention on ourselves rather than God. Many times this not only affects us but also the people around us. Prayer keeps us plugged into Jesus, which in turn energizes our faith into action. Amen!

"These were all commended for their faith, yet none of them received what had been promised" (Heb. 11:39). Do you feel a sense of disappointment? We read all week long about these Heroes of Faith, and now we learn that they didn't receive their promises when they expected them. What about Noah? His faith in God displayed spiritual strength, even though his actions made no sense to others. Remember how Abraham continued to press forward, always believing God's promise for a son? And think of all Moses went through as he led the Israelites out of captivity, putting total faith in God. Yesterday we focused on Gideon. The Lord used this Hero of Faith to lead the Israelite army to victory!

In your mind's eye, didn't these men deserve the fulfillment of God's promises? Why didn't they receive the promises? We must read the next verse: "God had planned something better for us so that only together with us would they be made perfect" (Heb. 11:40).

Real Life Facts

The final step in the gasoline supply chain is "The Pump." Gasoline gets transported to gas stations after the crude oil goes through the refining process. Cargo ships, trains, and tanker trucks transport gasoline to the locations where we buy gas; and then large hoses transfer the gasoline from the trucks to underground holding tanks. The last step in the process occurs when a driver comes to the gas station to fill his tank. The consumer puts the hose into his car's gas tank and pulls the trigger to start the flow of gasoline. Thankfully, modern-day gas pumps have an automatic device that releases the trigger and keeps the tank from overflowing.

Scripture Excavation

As you read Hebrews 11:39–40 together, what is God saying?

_____

_____

Read Hebrews 12:1–12. Why did God preface this block of scriptures with Hebrews 11:39–40?

_____

_____

Read Hebrews 12:2 again, and take time to consider every word in this verse. Who is the author and finisher of our faith? *God / Jesus*

_____

_____

THE OUTCOME

What does "finisher" of our faith mean?

_____

_____

In case you haven't guessed, Jesus is our final Hero of Faith. Read Philippians 2:1–11. What stands out in this passage? Based on this scripture, why is Jesus considered the author and finisher of our faith?

_____

_____

Hidden Treasures

If you were to present Jesus with a "Hero of Faith Badge," what would you say to those watching? Write out your speech, and really think about your audience as you do it.

_____

_____

Celebrating Treasured Gifts

It's your turn to make an analogy between the gas pump and the concept of "Prayer Fuels Faith." We made it through the gasoline supply chain. All week we focused on how prayer energizes faith into action. Have some of these insights increased your faith in God? Write a prayer of thanks to God.

_____

_____

_____

_____

_____

Reflection Pause

What a picture of our Christian lives! Just as the gas tank provides the energizing fuel to run our cars, Jesus gives us the energy we need to live out the Christian life. When we allow Jesus to fill our empty spiritual tanks every day, He gives us exactly what we need. Oh, how I love these real life analogies!

From now on, every time you put your hand on the gas pump, may you be reminded to ask Jesus to fill your spiritual tank to the top. Amen!

WEEK 7

THE CONTROL SYNDROME: CONSEQUENCES OF RUNNING AHEAD

Live by the Spirit, and you will not gratify the desires of the sinful nature.
—Galatians 5:16

When situations are out of your control, do you remain in control? What emotions raise their ugly heads during these times—frustration, impatience, anger, irritability? Do damaging words flow from your mouth? Often when life becomes difficult to manage, we simply throw in the towel. We need some practical ways to let go and let God take control of our lives. This week in "The Control Syndrome," we discover through the Word how to deal with issues that don't go according to plan. We focus on living in the Spirit and not in the flesh.

Prepare your heart to hear from the Lord each day. Ask Him to help you see areas where you need to relinquish your will and trust in Him.

The Gardener's Corner

Get ready for some fun as we visit the garden. The key to a garden's success lies with the gardener. He or she is the one who prepares the soil and plants the garden at just the right time. As the plants begin to grow, the gardener knows the perfect time to fertilize and water. A garden left unattended becomes susceptible to disease, bugs, weeds, mineral deficiencies, and drought.

This week we focus on the gardener and what he or she needs to create his or her masterpiece: a garden! Before any planting takes place, the gardener must pick a location and prepare the soil. Then after the seeds are planted, the gardener faces the challenges of weed invasion, bug infestation, unpredictable weather, and the appearance of fungus on the growing plants. So much to worry about!

Now let's learn how to let go and let God take control.

WEEK 7: DAY 1

SOIL OF THE SOUL

Live by the Spirit, and you will not gratify the desires of the sinful nature.
—Galatians 5:16

Why is it so difficult to walk in the Spirit and not in the flesh? "Live by the Spirit"—this sounds like a simple, almost easy way to live. But reality shows us this is not the case. In week 5, "Prayer from the Inside Out," it was explained that the Holy Spirit automatically sets up residence in a person's spiritual home the minute that person accepts Jesus as his or her Savior. But why doesn't this acceptance instinctively force us to make the right decisions for the rest of our lives?

God didn't design us to be robots! He designed us with a free will to choose between right and wrong. There is no doubt that the minute we accept Jesus as Lord and Savior we are choosing to say "yes" to His free gift of salvation. At that point, a believer's eternal position is secured in heaven with God, Jesus, and the Holy Spirit! But our daily walk with Jesus determines the condition of our relationship with Him. Spending time in the Word, prayer, worship, and fellowship with other believers helps develop a deeper connection with Jesus. Cultivating the heart with these disciplines prepares a believer to surrender everything to the Lord—husband, children, extended family, relationships, work, finances, illnesses—all of life. When we are able to relinquish control of our lives to God, it gives Him access to use us for His glory.

Have fun today preparing the "Soil of the Soul"!

Real Life Facts

The first step in planting a vegetable garden is choosing the right location. Sunlight is one of the major elements in a garden's success, because plants need a minimum of six hours of direct sunlight, although eight to ten hours will generate even greater results. Also, planting should not be too close to shrubs or trees, because their roots might invade the garden space, creating a natural competition for sun, water, and nutrients. Gardeners avoid low spots, because they are slow to warm in the spring, frost settles in them in the winter, and standing water can cause root rot.

Preparing the soil is essential for proper plant growth. First-time beds need the addition of organic material when the ground is tilled. To avoid creating large clumps, this should be done when the soil is dry. Humus and manure can be added to enrich the soil. For subsequent seasons, hand tilling is recommended to prevent disruption of earthworm activity.

Scripture Excavation

We head back to Genesis as we begin this week's study. Ask the Lord for a teachable spirit today—one that listens to and absorbs His Word. Begin by reading Genesis 2:4–17. We will break our focus into two parts: location and preparation.

Location

Identify any particulars regarding God's choice for the Garden of Eden's location. Do you think the specific location was important to God? Why or why not?

_____

_____

Where did God place the man He formed?

_____

_____

According to Genesis 2:9, what did God accomplish in the garden?

_____

_____

Here is the challenge. What are the "tree of life" and "the tree of the knowledge of good and evil"? Why are they important? Give other scriptures that might be significant in your explanation.

_____

_____

SOIL OF THE SOUL

Preparation

What did God do before any plants or herbs grew in the garden?
_____
_____

What else did God create for His beautiful garden (see vv.10–14)?
_____
_____

What job did God give to man?
_____
_____

What instructions did God give man?
_____
_____

It is important to note that up to this point the world experienced no sin, so the world resembled paradise. But that all changed in Genesis 3, because sin entered the world through Adam!

Hidden Treasures

After reading about planting and studying Genesis 2:4–17, what did you learn that you can apply in your own life?
_____
_____

Notice how God placed man in His garden to "tend and keep it." Has God placed you in a specific location or situation to "tend and keep it"? Are you resisting this "garden"? Perhaps it is the family in which you grew up, your spouse, your spouse's family, a child with a physical disability or difficult personality, a move or relocation, your work environment, a financial situation, or something more. Be honest and write your thoughts to the Lord.
_____
_____

Celebrating Treasured Gifts

As we conclude today's lesson, ask God to show you some areas in your life where you are trying to take control rather than releasing the situations to Him. Praise Him for your current "location." Ask Him to help you prepare the "Soil of your Soul" so that He can produce a crop that yields more than you ever could imagine. God has a beautiful garden planned for your life if you will allow Him to be the gardener of your soul.

___

___

___

___

___

___

Reflection Pause

I remember the first time I planted a garden. I read everything I could on making it a success. An excitement lay deep within my soul as I found the perfect place for my twenty-by-twenty-foot plot and started off on this new adventure. I just knew this ideal location would enable the plants to soak up the right amount of sun every day.

I purchased a variety of seeds, including lettuce, spinach, squash, beans, peppers, tomatoes, cantaloupe, and even watermelon. With all the knowledge I obtained before getting started, I could have written my own book called *Successful Gardening by Mama Mac*.

But it is amazing how quickly that know-it-all attitude left my mind when I took a big swing with my brand-new garden hoe. As I hit the ground, a vibration moved from the end of the hoe all the way up the handle until it reached my hands. I realized my hoe hadn't penetrated the soil but instead had hit rock—yes, the kind that takes a jackhammer to break. But wait, this hadn't been in the books! Yet I knew I needed enough dirt for the plants' roots to grow. What to do?

With the invincible attitude of a woman in her mid-twenties, I had the bright idea to get on my knees and scrape the rocks away with my hands. Needless to say, this plan got me nowhere. Looking back, I realize I was operating under a "control syndrome"! I wanted my gardening to go as I had planned.

In reality, this represented my life at the time. When things didn't go as I desired, I tried to force them to work according to my intentions. Just like the gardening experience, God placed "boulders" in my life because He had a better plan.

What about you? How do you handle the "boulders" that get in the way of your plans? Praise God for what He is teaching through these life situations!

WEEK 7: DAY 2

THE WAITING TIME

Night and day, whether he sleeps or gets up, the seed sprouts and grows, though he does not know how.

—Mark 4:27

The gardener must spend a lot of time and labor to make his garden grow to its full potential. The first reference to gardening in the Bible is in Genesis 2:15, "The Lord God took the man and put him in the Garden of Eden to work it and take care of it." This was a perfect garden! Sin had not fallen on the earth at this point. But the garden still required someone to tend and keep it.

God wants us to take care of the "gardens" in our lives. This hints at the fact that it takes time and effort to cultivate what God has given us. He has a plan, but we have to cultivate it. Do you agree with this statement, "A garden left unattended will fail to grow"? Why or why not?

Yesterday we discussed the importance of choosing a location with the right amount of direct sunlight. We also talked about the importance of preparing the soil before any seeds were planted. Now comes the planting. Poke a hole in the ground about a finger's length deep, and sprinkle three or four seeds into the hole (you don't want too many seeds competing in the same area). Cover the hole, and water heavily so the water reaches the seeds. Then comes the time of waiting, watching, and watering what you can't see. You trust that the seeds are germinating and taking root. And then one morning you walk out to water the garden (or dirt pit), and to your surprise, little green sprigs are poking up through the soil. The fruits of your labor are now exposed for the entire world to see!

Scripture Excavation

Let's dig into God's Word to discover the exciting lessons He wants to plant in our hearts today. Read Mark 4:26–29, the parable of the growing seed. What do you think about these verses?

_____
_____

What is the main subject of this parable?

_____
_____

What is the central truth of this parable?

_____
_____

Take a moment to make comparisons among this parable, a garden, and your life.

_____
_____
_____

Real Life Facts

Parables are real life stories, events, or analogies that convey a truth message. Jesus used these real life illustrations to create a new awareness and understanding of God's kingdom. Even today they capture the reader's attention, are easily remembered, and reveal truth to those who are prepared to receive their meanings. On the other hand, they make no sense to those who are not ready to receive God's truths. It is important to note that parables were designed to teach or illustrate a truth, not to be picked apart.

Hidden Treasures

Let's do something different today. Ask God to help you find new insights from His Word.

Expand your search of Mark 4:27 by reading 2 Peter 3:18. In both passages, the Greek word for "grow" is *auxano*, which means to grow; increase in plants, infants, or a multitude of people; or inward Christian growth. What is God saying in these verses?

_____
_____

Now read Mark 4:28 with John 12:24. What happens when a seed dies? What does God say about this?

___

___

Study Genesis 3:15 (NKJV), "And I will put enmity between you and the woman and between your seed and her Seed." Who is "her Seed" in this verse? What insights do you get from John 7:42 and Romans 1:1–6?

___

___

Celebrating Treasured Gifts

Recalling the central truth of the parable of the growing seed, write a summary of what God is teaching you through these verses. Thoughts to consider: How long did it take for God's promised Seed to sprout for the world to see? What about your gardening experience—do you patiently wait to see some growth? Do you trust what is happening before you see results? "The Waiting Time" is difficult, but it is a necessary part of learning to trust God. God has some powerful life lessons to teach us with this!

___

___

___

___

___

___

Reflection Pause

In my early adult years, one of my pastors asked me to serve on a committee at church. With excitement and enthusiasm, I said "yes." When I walked into the first meeting, I didn't know a soul. After about thirty minutes, I realized one person dominated the conversation; and the more she talked, the more frustrated I became. Thoughts ran through my mind such as, *There is no way I will serve on a team with this person!*

A few days later—without praying, I should add—I decided to withdraw my name from the committee. A sweet Christian friend quietly challenged me to ask the Lord to help me see that person through His eyes. I resolved to pray, but with little hope of changing my mind. After a few more meetings, I realized my previous annoyances had subsided. Amazingly, God started changing my heart, and I could then view my differences with her as a blessing. I grew to love her because of God's gift of love! You see, the more I tried to control the situation, the more annoyed I became with the committee, and the more frustrated I became with our purpose for serving the Lord. I wanted things to change immediately, but God needed to teach me about waiting on Him. Once I relinquished control over the situation and started praying, God changed me.

Are you dealing with circumstances out of your control? Is there someone at work who drives you crazy? Is there an area of your life that you haven't fully surrendered to God? Let God teach you through "The Waiting Time"!

WEEK 7: DAYS 3 AND 4

GARDEN INVASIONS— WEEDS AND PESTS

While everyone was sleeping, his enemy came and sowed weeds among the wheat.
—Matthew 13:25

You will sow much seed in the field but you will harvest little, because locusts will devour it.
—Deuteronomy 28:38

Did Adam experience weeds and pests in the Garden of Eden? We know God put Adam in the garden to work and take care of it. So did he use a specific method of prevention? This is a great "heaven question" to ask the Lord someday!

Where do weeds and insects originate? It seems like they come out of nowhere. As the planted seeds germinate and begin to break through the surface, weeds start popping up around the seedlings. The gardener must spend time and energy on weed control—pulling and cutting. Then there are the insects that seem to appear overnight. Some of the ugliest bugs alive can thrive in your garden. Take, for example, the huge tomato hornworm. It is fat, green, and spongy, and it will eat the leaves down to the stem in a matter of days. This pesky critter robs the plant of the nutrients it needs to produce fruit. Imagine the disappointment the gardener experiences when an annoying creepy-crawler eats his prize produce.

Today, ask the Lord to expose the "weed invasions" and "pest infestations" that are affecting your spiritual garden.

Real Life Facts[12]

Weeds are simply plants growing where they aren't wanted. As they grow, they compete with the garden plants for space, water, light, and nutrients. If not eliminated, they eventually will take over the garden, crowding out the vegetables.

Certain bugs can wipe out a garden in a matter of hours. Here are a few examples:

- Cabbage Aphids work in large populations, feeding on the undersides of leaves.
- Asparagus Beetles show up just as the asparagus spears are emerging from the soil.
- Potato Leaf Hoppers feed on hundreds of cultivated and wild plants. Their piercing mouths extract the plant's juices. They inject saliva that prevents growth.

Scripture Excavation

Today we examine two lessons designed to help with the "control syndrome." First, we dig into the parable of the weeds, and you will be asked to make note of the "weeds" that continually invade your life. Second, we look at some of the scriptures that refer to locusts and other insects.

Begin by asking the Lord to open your mind and heart that you might acknowledge the "pests" zapping the energy from your walk with Jesus.

Weeds

Read the parable of the wheat and tares in Matthew 13:24–30 and the explanation of the parable of the tares in Matthew 13:36–43. A *tare* is another word for *weed*. Give a description of each:

- Sower of the good seed

_____

_____

- Good seed

_____

_____

- Tares

_____

_____

- Sower of the tares

_____

_____

GARDEN INVASIONS—WEEDS AND PESTS

- The harvest

- The reapers

What is the central truth of the parable of the wheat and tares?

It is important to understand that as tares grow they look like wheat but they are very poisonous. It is not until their final stage of growth that the farmer can tell the wheat from the tares. How can you apply this parable to your life?

Are you responsible for the tares growing in your garden? Explain.

Pests

Read Joel 1:1–12 and Deuteronomy 28:38–47. What did you learn about locusts?

Throughout the Bible, God uses locusts to represent His judgment on the Israelites. Give examples from these scriptures to support this.

Were the Israelites responsible for God's actions toward them? Why or why not?

According to these scriptures, are you responsible for the "locusts" that attack your luscious "garden"? Explain your answer.

_____

_____

Hidden Treasures

As you probably noticed, today's lesson consists of Day 3 and Day 4. It is imperative to study these analogies together to understand their differences. Now as we move to personal applications, open your heart to God's Word and truth messages.

Tares look like wheat, but there are other weeds that obviously look like they don't belong. Read the "Real Life Facts" section again to refresh your memory on weeds. Are there any weeds that need to be picked in your spiritual "garden"? What actions do you need to take to get rid of those unwanted "plants"?

_____

_____

Did you grasp the analogy of a garden attacked by locusts and God's judgment for the disobedient? The damage a swarm of locusts can do to an entire crop is unbelievable. God's judgment is even greater. What does God call us to do when we have been disobedient?

_____

_____

To understand God's heart on repentance, you must read further—Joel 2:12–25. What do verses 12–13 say about how the Lord responds to a repentant heart?

_____

_____

Now . . . drum role, please! What is God saying to you through Joel 2:25? (I love this!)

_____

_____

Celebrating Treasured Gifts

Take a moment to be honest with the Lord. Have you been trying to control some areas in your life that the Lord is calling you to release to Him? Pour your heart out to the Lord, and ask forgiveness and for His mercy and grace beyond your understanding. Nothing is too big for Him!

_____

_____

GARDEN INVASIONS—WEEDS AND PESTS

_____
_____
_____
_____
_____

Reflection Pause

I must continue with the story of my first gardening experience. As the vegetables started to appear on my plants, I became somewhat proud of my accomplishment. One morning I went out to water and noticed some big, ugly bugs all over my squash plants. What were they? Where did they come from? What did I do about them?

I ran into the house and called my husband. With a chuckle in his voice, he said, "Honey, don't worry—they're just squash bugs. There are products available to get rid of them."

I immediately went to the store, purchased an organic pesticide, and started spraying my beautiful squash plants. It's amazing how well it worked.

Can you see a spiritual application in this story?

WEEK 7: DAY 5

COMPANION PLANTING

I (Paul) planted the seed, Apollos watered it, but God made it grow.

—1 Corinthians 3:6

Why does God call His children to work as one in the body of Christ? Why does He command us to form a unit, knowing full well our different personalities, traits, and backgrounds? Have you ever said to the Lord, "Are you kidding? I can't serve on this committee with this person"? More than likely we have all said this at one time or another. But God wants us to view each other as gifts from Him.

Take, for example, your family. Let's say your vegetable garden needs a fence to keep out predators. The whole family decides to work on this project, and initially everyone enjoys working together. But then you notice one member taking more breaks than the others and not working to his full potential. No one says a word to the slacker, but frustration with his lack of commitment is obvious.

One morning after the fence is finished, you walk outside to water the garden and notice that a part of the fence is down. Overnight, the flourishing garden was stripped of much of its bounty. Upon closer inspection, you realize that the fence section that collapsed didn't have as many support nails as the other segments. You guessed it: the slacker! In his laziness and unconcern, he thought no one would notice. Now what to do? Throw him out of the family and disown him? No, you decide to work through the situation together.

It is the same with God's family. We are God's gift to one another, but we have different talents, abilities, weaknesses, and personalities. The Lord uses these to bring strength to the body of Christ and share the message of salvation through Jesus.

Real Life Facts[13]

Some vegetables grow better in the company of other plants. Some plants repel harmful insects, while others attract useful bugs; and many enhance the growth and flavor of their companions. This type of planting helps bring a balanced environment to your garden, but it is important to know which plants do something good and which ones create adverse effects. A few examples are marigolds, which are beneficial throughout the garden; beans, which are good with rosemary; cucumbers, which are bad with onions; and roses, which are good with garlic.

Scripture Excavation

Read 1 Corinthians 3:5–9. What is God saying to you through these verses?

_____

_____

What are some spiritual applications for the words "plant" and "water"?

_____

_____

Keeping this block of scriptures in the forefront of your mind, read 1 Corinthians 12:12–31. Write a summary of what you sense God is saying to His children.

_____

_____

It is interesting to take note of the very next chapter, 1 Corinthians 13. What is the main focus of this chapter? Do you believe that God strategically "planted" this theme after the topic of unity in the body? Why or why not?

_____

_____

Are there other scriptures about unity that you want to share?

_____

_____

Hidden Treasures

Do you find it difficult to serve on a team or committee with people who are different from you? Maybe they dress differently, your personalities clash, or you are on opposite ends of the spectrum in your ways of thinking.

Perhaps, in your opinion, they see life circumstances through a glass half-empty while you see situations through a glass half-full. What are some things you can do to realize the value of these differences? Ask yourself: what is my goal—to get along with this person/team or to control the decisions?

_____

_____

Think back to the examples of companion planting. What are some examples of God planting "companions" in your life? Have fun with this question!

_____

_____

Celebrating Treasured Gifts

Pour out your heart to the Lord, asking Him to help you accept His control instead of trying to do things yourself.

_____

_____

_____

_____

_____

Reflection Pause

Garlic is a wonderful herb to grow in the garden. Its presence protects against harmful insects. But by nature, it is an aggressive plant. A gardener can expect it to attempt a takeover. It spreads by producing seed heads that fall to the ground and sprout up as new plants. Its roots suck the nutrients out of the soil, leaving hard clumps of dirt that are of no use to the other plants around it. It must be controlled!

Just like a gardener controls the spread of the garlic plant, we must allow the True Gardener—God—to have control of the seeds and roots growing in our spiritual lives. We must give God access to cut, chop, or pull the bitter roots that tend to take over and rob us of our joy.

Ask God to reveal any bitter roots that are sucking the nutrients from your spiritual life. Allow the Lord to be your Gardener and cultivate your life for His glory!

Warning: Don't fall into the trap of the "control syndrome." It will zap all of your energy. God desires for us to surrender it all to Him so He can accomplish His purposes in our lives. Look forward to letting go and letting God take over!

WEEK 8

ROADBLOCKS AHEAD: CAUTION— DIVERSIONS ALONG THE WAY

Be self-controlled and alert. Your enemy the devil prowls around like a roaring lion looking for someone to devour.

—1 Peter 5:8

Be encouraged, we're coming to the end of the study! Together we will finish strong. These last few chapters are seasoned with the spices needed to make this study complete. Keep it up! God has sweet blessings for each of us to behold.

Frustration—how do you handle this emotion? When plans don't go the way you expect, how do you react? If unmet expectations are not dealt with properly, they can manifest themselves into anger, impatience, or even depression. These reactions could result in your decision to give up or throw in the towel. Keeping your eyes on Jesus is the key to handling all disappointments.

It is important to remember that sometimes the Lord allows roadblocks because He has a different route for you to take. On the other hand, some of our diversions are self-induced because of choices we make. Then again, the enemy Satan constantly works to halt God's plans and purposes for His children. God has many exciting things to teach each of us through "Roadblocks Ahead." Take time to pray so your heart is prepared to receive spiritual wisdom!

Road Construction 101

Reflect on the following scenario. You have a very important meeting at eight in the morning, so you estimate the time needed to drive, park, and walk to your destination. Leaving the house on time has given you a feeling of accomplishment. With confidence, you choose the best time-saving route, but as you drive you notice a build-up of traffic ahead of you. To your dismay, you realize that the two-lane road has narrowed to one lane due to construction. Needless to say, there is an unanticipated glitch in your plans.

This week we look at the analogy between road construction and life's roadblocks. We'll examine the details of road construction—plans, detours, road-sign changes, traffic, and potholes. Ask God to show you some dynamic life lessons as you study each day of "Roadblocks Ahead."

WEEK 8: DAY 1

FORKS IN THE ROAD

I am the way, the truth, and the life. No one comes to the Father except through me.
—John 14:6 NKJV

Do you enjoy making decisions? Have you ever experienced one of those "mind" debates—you know, those conversations where you try to convince yourself to do one thing over another while actually talking out loud?

Think about the cereal aisle at the grocery store. A few years ago selecting a cereal wasn't that difficult. Now there is an overabundance of brands and choices. Sometimes I go up and down this aisle saying things like, "This one tastes good, but what about that one? That brand is healthy, but my kids like this one better." Are you tracking with me? Every day we are bombarded with decisions!

Can you remember the last time you left the directions to your destination at home? You "kind of" recalled how to get there, so you decided not to go back for the map. But when you approached a fork in the road, you had no idea which way to go. The "I thinks" took over, as both paths looked correct. You were then driving on instinct and being "directionally challenged." Every turn you made took you a little farther from your destination. You were kicking yourself for not turning around to get the map.

Choices, choices, choices! Oh, the Lord has exciting things ahead for us today in our study. Grab God's "Book of Directions," and let's go!

Real Life Facts

The construction of a new road requires an engineering and environmental assessment. This includes an alignment study to identify the most efficient route for the new roadway. It is vital to detect any environmental impacts and create an improvement plan that considers everything.

Spiritual Excavation

There is no better place to begin this week's study than with the road to Damascus. Read Acts 9:1–22. For background information on Saul (Paul), read Acts 7:54–8:3. What was Paul's objective at this time?

_____

_____

In those days it was not unusual to go by two different names. When Paul was with the Jews he was called Saul. But among the Gentiles he went by the name Paul, which means "small one." For our study we will use "Paul." What spiritual parallels do you see in Acts 9:1–4 to John 14:6?

_____

_____

In John 14:6 and Acts 9:2, the Greek word for the root word "way," according to *Strong's Concordance of the Bible*, is *hodos*.[14] This means a traveler's way, journey, traveling, a traveled road, or road. Isn't it interesting how God works? This same phrase—the way Paul described "followers of Christ"—contains the exact words Jesus used for Himself in John 14:6. Ironically, Jesus met Paul on "a traveled road" as the tax collector "journeyed" to arrest any who were of the Way.

Restate Acts 9:5–9 in your own words. For further insights, read Acts 22:1–11. Again, look for any unique symbolisms within these blocks of scriptures (hint: John 1:6–9).

_____

_____

Take a few minutes to analyze Acts 9:10–19. What spiritual insights do you see in the fact that Jesus sent Paul to "Straight Street?" This Greek word for "straight" is *euthus,* which means straightforward, upright, true, sincere.

_____
_____

Hidden Treasures

Let's do a recap of what we excavated in the Scriptures today. As a tax collector, Paul grew angry toward the followers of Christ. He threatened them and even murdered some of them. His persecution toward believers continued to intensify. But God's plan to use Paul for His glory came at a perfect time. Re-read Acts 9:15 and Acts 22:12–16. Now let's get real! Can you remember a time when you traveled down the "wrong road"? How did Jesus halt you on your journey and point you in the right Way? At the time, did you recognize Jesus re-routing your direction to His Way? Take time to write your heartfelt testimony. This is a powerful opportunity to relive Jesus' hand on your life and praise Him for how He personally drew you to Himself.

_____
_____
_____
_____

Do you, as a follower of the Way, believe God has a plan for your life? Do you trust that God desires to use you for His kingdom? Oh, sister, run to Him! Jesus is the Way, the Truth, and the Life. No one comes to the Father except through Jesus. Amen!

_____
_____
_____
_____

Celebrating Treasured Gifts

Look back at the traffic sign at the beginning of today's lesson. Notice an arrow represents the main route with other roads leading away from it. Now think of the main road as a "spiritual road" that represents the Way. As we journey through life, we find many opportunities to take a wrong turn. These side roads may lead in the wrong direction or take us the long way around to our destination. But when we follow our map (God's

Word) we travel the Way the Master Engineer designed, and it helps us to avoid rough roads, potholes, and broken bridges. So each time you come to a "fork in the road," how will you determine which way to go?

_____
_____
_____
_____
_____
_____

Reflection Pause

Doubt, fear, decisions. *Oh, God what should I do?*

Have you experienced this thought? Can you recall a time when you were gripped with fear because of a decision that needed to be made? We've all been there at one time or another. Personally, I wish God would give me the answer straight up. A billboard would be nice! Or how about an e-mail? This would work wonderfully—imagine opening your inbox and receiving a message from God!

Ummm . . . why doesn't He work this way? As believers we have the privilege to talk to God 24/7. Anytime! He is there waiting to listen, act, and commune with us. He desires an ongoing communication with His children. If you are a parent, you can understand. He doesn't want us to just call on Him during emergencies. Yes, He is there during those times when we need crisis counseling, but He wants us to come to Him for everything.

I remember as a young child hearing my grandmother talk about praying for parking spots at the grocery store. She said sometimes she would get a spot close to the front and other times in "the boondocks." It didn't matter where she parked, she always thanked God. She continued to tell me that He was in control. In my child's mind, this seemed odd. But in reality she displayed to me an ongoing, daily-seeking, trusting, and living relationship with Jesus. Oh, what a blessing to watch that woman live her life for Him! In her later years, when my grandmother's driving days were over, I called her on a regular basis. Often when I asked about her day she replied with these words: "I'm in my Prayer Chair."

Tears are rolling down my cheeks as I write this. You see, my grandmother showed me what it was like to have a daily connection with Jesus—not based on what I could *do* for Him, but just on being *with* Him. I thank God for a grandmother who displayed such a living, breathing relationship to her family. I wonder if one day when I get to heaven I will be able to hear a replay of all the prayers she prayed over me.

When you are faced with a "fork in the road," pray, pray, pray!

WEEK 8: DAY 2

DETOURS IN LIFE

When they came to the border of Mysia, they tried to enter Bithynia, but the Spirit of Jesus would not allow them to.

—Acts 16:7

*D*etours. *Deviations. Alternate routes.* When you read those words you might think, *Not again. This is not what I planned!* Why do detours happen?

For example, your family takes a trip to visit relatives halfway across the country and you've been in the car for twenty hours. It's getting late, and there's only thirty minutes until you reach your destination. The kids sound like a broken record: "When are we going to get there?" Needless to say, you are exhausted, but the end is in sight. Then in the distance you see a blinking yellow light. As you get closer, you notice a large sign with an arrow pointing away from the direction you want to take. When the words come into focus, they read:

Road Closed. Detour 20 miles.

Frustration builds as your youngest cries that he needs to go to the bathroom. For a split second, you consider going around the sign to continue straight ahead to your destination. But taking a deep breath, you realize there is only one choice: to follow the detour sign.

Such is life! Sometimes it seems everything is in order, including our plans for the future, and then something unexpected happens. We stumble on a great detour in life. Our current path now seems obscure, and our destination is out of sight. We are faced with a choice: either accept the detour with grace or react with bitterness and anger.

Detours—you have to take them, even when they are inconvenient!

Real Life Facts

Why "detours"? One way to define "detour" is a deviation from a direct course of action or a roundabout course of action.[15] Roads occasionally need to be repaired or resurfaced with fresh materials because of heavy traffic and the weather. While the work is being done, traffic is rerouted for the construction workers' safety. Detours are unavoidable.

Scripture Excavation

Yesterday we studied Paul's experience with Jesus on the road to Damascus—the way they met face to face, and how Jesus directed Paul in the right Way. When you read Acts 9–16, you see Paul lived the rest of his life spreading the message of salvation through Jesus. But it didn't happen without some bumps in the road. In fact, he frequently dealt with detours along the way. Read Acts 15:30–16:5. What was Paul's original plan, and what blockade did he hit?

_____

_____

What happened as a result of this disagreement?

_____

_____

How did God use this outcome to further His kingdom (see Acts 15:41 and Acts 16:5)?

_____

_____

Explain Acts 16:6–10. Who forbid Paul and Silas from going into Asia? Look at a map of Paul's first and second journeys, and notice Paul and Silas had an agenda. But the Holy Spirit detoured their plans. Why do you think the Holy Spirit changed their route? This is a very important question that affects us even today.

_____

_____

Hidden Treasures

Notice Paul and Silas' attitudes. They didn't complain or rebel. They didn't become upset or act in a selfish way. They simply obeyed without resisting the change to their agenda. They desired to go wherever Jesus led them. So when their path to Asia detoured, they followed the road signs and didn't veer off course. We know God is always true to His Word and what He says will come to pass, right?

Read Acts 9:15–16. How is this verse being fulfilled in Acts 16:6–10? This is really exciting!

_____

_____

Celebrating Treasured Gifts

Are you experiencing a "life stop" right now? Are you confused about why God is allowing this in your life? Learn to praise Him in the midst of the moment. Praise Him! He knows best, and He has a mighty plan. Thank Him for teaching you to trust Him through the situation that doesn't make sense to you. Ask God to prepare you for those times where you seem to freeze in your tracks. Go a step further and pray for others you know who may be experiencing tough times. Pray for them to trust God and realize He is in control.

_____

_____

_____

_____

_____

Reflection Pause

"What? Are you kidding me? This really messes things up!" Have you ever said those words? How do you handle detours that make no sense at all? Those in ministry are not immune to these changes. Recently, I experienced one of these moments.

I schedule my speaking events months in advance, and due to some unusual circumstances, a church cancelled an event with me. At first I experienced disappointment, but a couple of days later I received a call from a woman wanting to know how to build a women's ministry team. She said when she Googled "women's retreats in Texas," Reflective Life Ministries appeared. She went on to say that her church is located in a small Texas town with a population of 525. God stirred the hearts of six women to begin a women's ministry, but they didn't know where or how to start. As we continued to visit, I realized that God's hand was in this conversation. We both knew God had connected us for His purposes to be accomplished. As a result, she asked me to come speak at a kickoff event for the ladies. And, wouldn't you know, the only time that worked in their schedule happened to be the date that had opened up for me two days before. Wow, only God!

The day arrived for the kickoff. Driving into this small town, I could feel the Lord's presence in a very powerful way. God confirmed in my heart that the Holy Spirit allowed the disappointing detour to rearrange my schedule. Obviously, God desired for me to share my passion for Jesus at a quaint church in a little Texas town with fifty-four ladies. These women were hungry to hear God's Word and excited for a fresh experience with Jesus.

Yes, God allows detours for a reason!

WEEK 8: DAY 3

THE WORK ZONE

About midnight Paul and Silas were praying and singing hymns to God, and the prisoners were listening to them.

—Acts 16:25

How do you handle unforeseen life events? Do you let them affect you physically? Do your emotions skyrocket? Is there a spiritual pause in your walk with Jesus? Or maybe you view unexpected situations as a way to draw nearer to God. You might see these experiences as an opportunity to live out Philippians 4:13 (NKJV), "I can do everything through Christ who strengthens me."

Learning to live in victory with Jesus despite our circumstances should be one of our prayers as Christians. The enemy tries to entice believers into believing that they are immune to persecution. False! Christians are targets. Not because the enemy can snatch us from Jesus' hand, but because we are Jesus' hands and feet here on earth. The enemy works hard to encumber our relationships with Jesus so that we fail to accomplish God's purposes.

God uses these difficult times in our lives to refine us, perfect our faith, and make us more like Jesus. They can be compared to work zones in road construction. One day you're driving down the highway and come upon a sign like the one at the beginning of today's study:

Road Work Ahead

This should immediately warn you to slow down. In fact, if you speed in a work zone, the fines are doubled. Why? Because there are workers on-site whose lives are at risk. The slower traffic is for the driver's safety as well.

Today, look forward to new spiritual insights as we focus on "The Work Zone" in a Christian's life.

Real Life Facts—Tips for Driving in Work Zones[16]

- Expect the unexpected—reduced speeds, changed traffic lanes, and workers.
- Slow down—speeding is one of the major causes of work-zone crashes.
- Don't tailgate—keep a safe distance from the car in front of you. The most common crash in a highway work zone is the rear-end collision.
- Keep a safe distance—between you and construction workers.
- Pay attention to the signs—they are there to help you move safely through the work zone.
- Obey the flagger—he knows the best way to move traffic safely in the work zone.
- Stay alert and minimize distractions—focus your full attention on the road; avoid changing radio stations or using a cell phone while driving in a work zone.
- Keep up with the traffic flow—merge smoothly into lanes; don't slow down to gaze at roadwork equipment or crews.
- Schedule enough time to drive safely—do your homework, and check Web sites for details on road construction areas.
- Be patient and stay calm—work zones are designed to improve road conditions for you and other drivers.

Scripture Excavation

We are working our way through Paul's life in the book of Acts. Day 1 focused on Paul's conversion on the road to Damascus. In Day 2 we studied how the Holy Spirit forbade Paul from entering Asia. This detour directed Paul into Macedonia, where he preached Jesus' message to the Gentiles. Today, Paul is in the spotlight again. Because of Acts 16:1–10, he knew the Holy Spirit already had drawn a map for the journey. As he and Silas continued through Macedonia, they hit a "work zone" area. I can't wait another minute to see what God has prepared for us to learn today!

Read Acts 16:11–40. In verse 16, where were Paul and Silas headed and why?

_____

_____

Who met them and what happened?

_____

_____

In Acts 16:16–22, who do you think was really behind the slave girl's work? Who was behind the actions of the slave girl's owners and why?

_____
_____

What was the result of Paul's persecution in Acts 16:23–24?

_____
_____

Explain Paul and Silas's attitude in Acts 16:25–40. Why do you think they possessed this outlook on their lives and their situation?

_____
_____

Who watched Paul and Silas while they were in prison, and how did their attitudes affect the watchers? Why did God want these people to participate in Paul and Silas's prison experience?

_____
_____

Hidden Treasures

This exercise is going to be fun and challenging! Look back at the "Real Life Facts" section and think about Paul and Silas's prison experience as their spiritual work zone. Now do a comparison between the tips for driving in a work zone and what happened during Paul and Silas's imprisonment. Pick three or four tips to compare. This is a challenging assignment with splashes of humor interspersed in the process. Be creative and have fun!

_____
_____
_____

Celebrating Treasured Gifts

Maybe you are in the middle of a spiritual work zone right now. Is the Lord working on resurfacing, widening, or smoothing something in your life? Thank Him for those work zones, because He allows them for your own good.

_____
_____

_____

_____

_____

_____

Reflection Pause

Expect the unexpected! Paul and Silas were not immune to difficult situations. In fact, as they were on their way to church to pray they were hit with another diversion. God allowed it because He had a special "work zone" He needed to construct.

As believers serving the Lord, we must be prepared for the unexpected things in life. If we keep our eyes on Jesus, He will lead us safely through the spiritual work zones we encounter. Is God redirecting your path to a different spiritual work zone? Are you preparing for the work God needs you to accomplish for Him? Like Paul and Silas, expect the unexpected!

WEEK 8: DAY 4

WATCH FOR POTHOLES

While Paul was waiting for them in Athens, he was greatly distressed to see that the city was full of idols.

—Acts 17:16

You're driving on a familiar highway. Praise music fills the car with a sense of peace and joy. This road is one you have traveled time and again. You almost feel as if you can set the car on autopilot, take a nap, and arrive at your destination. The road appears to be in excellent condition. In fact, six months prior, the county resurfaced it with asphalt and new road stripes.

Suddenly, you drive over a pothole. As you feel the jolt, you hear a loud sound that is reminiscent of something you would hear on the Fourth of July. The steering wheel starts jerking as you slowly veer the car off to the side of the road. Needless to say, one of your tires didn't survive the bump into the pothole.

How did the pothole form? The road appeared to be in top-notch condition, at least on the surface. What caused the road to break down in that particular spot? Today we look at potholes in roads and compare them to the "potholes" in our spiritual lives. Get ready for some eye-opening experiences as we study the importance of a firm foundation.

Real Life Facts

Potholes may occur because the base material under the pavement is not compacted properly. This causes the rocks under the pavement to loosen and shift, which in turn, creates cracks at the surface. Water seeps through the cracks and eventually breaks apart the surface material. Potholes can also form because the soil under the roadway swells as it absorbs water and shrinks as it dries out. This repetitive process creates cracks in the pavement, allows water to seep through the cracks, and then breaks the driving surface apart. Typically, chemical lime is used to treat the soil to reduce the "swelling" potential. But when you get right down to it, poor foundations and water create potholes.

Scripture Excavation

Remember Paul and Silas's detour while they were on their way to Asia? The Holy Spirit forbade them from preaching the message of salvation in the province of Asia. To get a better understanding of this journey, look at a map of Paul's second journey. God re-routed their second trip in a northwestern direction to Troas. This is where Paul heard the call to go into Macedonia—the right place at the right time! God promised Paul that he would be a light to the Gentiles, and now Paul and Silas were venturing into an unknown land with the Holy Spirit as their tour guide!

Following the map of Paul's second journey, we see that they moved through the towns of Macedonia—Samothrace, Neapolis, Philippi, and Thessalonica. The disciples experienced ups and downs in their ministry. Just when discouragement was about to set in with Paul and Silas, what did God do, according to Acts 17:10–15?

_____

_____

Read Acts 17:16–33. Describe Athens at this time.

_____

_____

In verse 23, why was Paul so disturbed by the inscription he found on an altar?

_____

_____

Hidden Treasures

Let's do some more excavation. I know you are pumped for another daring adventure, so here goes! Compare and contrast road construction, Paul's second journey, and your own spiritual walk with Jesus. Add any points that make God's Word relevant to you today. Remember, a solid foundation is what makes or breaks the surface of the road. Ready, set, go!

_____

_____

Celebrating Treasured Gifts

God's timing is always perfect. He is the best encourager! He gives us everything we need to build a strong and steady foundation—one that will not crumble in times of stress or through worldly pressures. Take time to praise Him for providing you with all you need to construct a solid path so that you don't stumble into life's potholes. Maybe your life needs resurfacing. Confess it to Jesus. Give Him access to fill the potholes with His love, strength, grace, and mercy. Bless you today, my friend!

_____

_____

_____

_____

_____

Reflection Pause

Paul received encouragement from God through the believers who took care of him and provided him with safety. It's almost like Paul was driving down a spiritual highway at full speed. The road surface appeared to be in excellent condition, when suddenly, he hit a pothole! The Athenians seemed to be a religious group of people. But the problem is, they didn't build their foundation on the true Word of God. As a result, leaks in their religious thinking made it possible for false teachings and idol worship to seep in and spread.

WEEK 8: DAY 5

CAUTION: SLOW TRAFFIC AHEAD!

"Quick!" he said to me. "Leave Jerusalem immediately, because they will not accept your testimony about me."

—Acts 22:18

Imagine yourself driving in five o'clock traffic. As you approach an intersection, the light turns red. Frustrated and annoyed from your hectic day, you reluctantly come to a stop. Words flood your mind that you know are not pleasing to the Lord.

While waiting for the light to change, you glance at the car beside you. In the driver's seat is a woman talking to herself with her hand up in the air. She looks like she might be trying to catch something. Again, you see her grip the air, but this time at her ear, then in front of her face, and suddenly she claps her hands together. With a determined look she once again smacks her hands together. But this time her facial expression changes to excitement as her fist raises and her lips mouth, "Yes!"

You find yourself staring at her with a "what in the world is she doing?" feeling. You can't help but laugh when her eyes meet yours and she realizes you were watching her. Shock shows on her face as she gives you a swift wave before turning her head. Needless to say, your negative attitude is gone. In fact, it is actually replaced with a lighthearted feeling the rest of the evening.

OK, I must admit: I am the lady doing the weird hand jive! Driving down the road I realized a mosquito had taken up residence in my car. He decided to use my head as target practice. He would build up speed and dive right at my ear, just like a fighter jet swooping in at his enemy. I knew my chance to squash the pest came when I stopped at the intersection. Well, you know the rest of the story.

Driving away from the scene, a thought popped into my head. Maybe the other driver needed that little bit of silliness to lighten her day. In fact, I prayed for God to use this stoplight situation to bring her joy. It might sound funny to pray for something like this, but I believe God uses life experiences to remind us of Him and what is important.

Caution lights, yield signs, warning symbols. How do these signals affect you as you drive? Let's say you teach a Sunday school class and need to arrive at church early to set up the classroom. On the drive you approach a busy intersection, and the traffic light turns from green to yellow. Now what? Do you step on the gas to make it through the intersection while the light is still yellow? Or do you stop even though you know it probably will make you late? Fortunately, you choose to heed the warning, avoiding a collision with a dump truck that barrels through the intersection.

Just like these traffic signs and signals, God alerts His children of danger in the world. It is important for us to stay in tune with the Lord so that we can see His warning signs as we go through each day. The more we seek Him, the more our eyes are opened to His directions and guidance for our life's journey.

Today, prepare your heart and mind to hear from the Lord. And don't forget, when you study a block of scriptures, God often gives you an opportunity to practice what you are learning. He wants you to move head knowledge to heart knowledge.

Real Life Facts

- Congestion on the roads in the United States is growing. Result: slower traffic!
- Many U.S. highways are approaching middle age and need repair, which causes an increased number of work zones. Result: slower traffic!

Scripture Excavation

Let's pick up where we left off yesterday. Paul encountered Jesus on the road to Damascus, and as a result, changed his plans, which were to persecute the Jews who were preaching about salvation through Jesus. Paul came to trust in Jesus and immediately began sharing Christ's message with others.

Now we focus on Paul's ministry. To fully grasp his experience in Jerusalem, read Acts 21–22:11. Write a heading and short summary for each of the following blocks of scriptures. Note all the warning signs given to Paul and his responses to them.

- Acts 21:1–16

CAUTION: SLOW TRAFFIC AHEAD!

- Acts 21:15–25

_____

_____

- Acts 21:26–36

_____

_____

- Acts 21:37–22:1–21

_____

_____

Hidden Treasures

Look at the scriptures in Acts again. Can you find any similarities between the warnings to Paul from fellow believers and the title of today's lesson, "Caution: Slow Traffic Ahead"? List at least three examples.

_____

_____

Do you think Paul did wrong by not following his friends' advice? Explain your answer.

_____

_____

Why did God give Paul these warning signs?

_____

_____

Celebrating Treasured Gifts

Praise God for the warning signs He puts in your path. Ask Him to help you see beyond the diversion. Thank Jesus for being the Way, the Truth, and the Life! Write out a song of praise, a poem, or a letter exalting the Lord for being with you twenty-four hours a day, seven days a week.

_____

_____

_____

_____

_____

_____

Reflection Pause

When you pass a "slow traffic" road sign, does it mean you are to stop, turn around, and not move forward? No, but now you are prepared for something ahead. God does the same thing with us. He knows what is in front of us, and in His tenderness He gives caution signs to forewarn us. Our role is to stay focused on God so we recognize when He is speaking to us.

In this week's scripture, we learned that Paul knew God's purpose for him. Paul stayed focused on God so he could pursue His objective no matter what the cost. God didn't want Paul to stop sharing Christ's message with others, so He provided information for him on his journey. Watch for God's words of caution in life. They might be the encouragement you need!

Look for the diversions the Lord puts in your day to bring a smile to your face. Ask Him to help you keep things in perspective. When you experience a bad day, look for ways to take the focus off the situation and put it on God instead. Or maybe you can be the one God uses to help someone else make it through the day. Let's say the cashier at the grocery store has a sour look on her face as she scans your groceries. You have a choice: You can respond back with a similarly unpleasant attitude, or you can smile, say a quick prayer for her, and give her a word of encouragement. You might be the diversion God uses to move her from focusing on herself to thinking of Jesus!

WEEK 9

FIT FOR JESUS: GET UP! GET OUT! GET GOING!

Whoever claims to live in him must walk as Jesus did.

—1 John 2:6

What is one of the most proclaimed New Year's resolutions? You probably guessed it: to exercise on a regular basis. At one time or another, most of us have made this resolution. Usually, the goal is to exercise several times a week. With enthusiasm and purpose, you set up a regular workout schedule for the next few months. The first day, the gym is packed; and you realize you are not the only one who made this pledge.

Your dedication motivates you through the first month. But in succeeding months, one excuse leads to the next as your to-do list takes priority. As a result, your trips to the gym happen less frequently; and weeks later, you realize your resolution has blown away with the wind. Frustration replaces the enthusiasm you once possessed for working out.

Why do we make commitments and fail to follow through with them? What gets in our way? Isn't this like the Christian life? We vow to read God's Word daily, but over time, something gets in the way.

This week we focus our attention on Jesus, our Lord and Savior. We look at His characteristics of dedication, devotion, steadfastness, responsibility, and diligence. The goal this week is to grab hold of the importance of finishing the race well. So get up, get out, and get going!

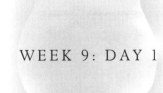

WEEK 9: DAY 1

TRAINING FOR THE PRIZE

We continually remember before our God and Father your work produced by faith, your labor prompted by love, and your endurance inspired by hope in our Lord Jesus Christ.
—1 Thessalonians 1:3

You are almost there! We have only two weeks left in our study. You are doing a great job! How does it feel to know that you honored your commitment? Keep it up, sister-friend—let's finish this race together. Imagine our arms raised to the sky as we cross the finish line shouting, "Praise be to God! It is so much fun 'Living for Jesus and Loving It.'" Can you hear the cheer of the saints as God says, "Well done, good and faithful servant"?

Today's study is about preparing ourselves for spiritual competitions. These life contests have some essential preparation elements, and just like any type of exercise or sports event, basic training is fundamental. A marathon runner preps for months before running a twenty-six-mile race. Swimmers practice daily. A biker rides for miles at a time to prime himself for a cycling event. If an athlete misses a week of training, it is sometimes easy to find excuses for not getting back into the routine. At that point the athlete is almost back where he or she started.

Regular workouts keep the body in shape for a competition. The same is true of our Christian lives. We must continually stay in a training mode—praying, reading the Word, spending time with other believers, praising and worshiping Jesus, going to church, etc. If we stop our spiritual workouts, we will not be prepared for life's spiritual competitions.

Real Life Facts

Training for an athletic competition requires discipline. Regular exercise helps an athlete achieve strength and endurance, while sporadic exercise can cause injury and soreness, which could lead to discontinuing the program. Setting workout goals is also important to attaining success. The competitor must identify his training program, fuel his body with proper nutrients, and know when to rest.

Scripture Excavation

Have you ever done a study on 1 Thessalonians? With excitement, I announce this book as our focus for the week. Paul is the author of this book, and Silas and Timothy are with him. This letter encourages believers to walk in a manner worthy of Jesus Christ. Read 1 Thessalonians 1. This short chapter is packed with spiritual training guidelines. If you received a letter like this, how would verse 2 encourage you?

Focus in on 1 Thessalonians 1:3. Write out the three areas Paul remembered:

1. *Work produced by faith*

2. *Labor prompted by Love.*

3. *Endurace inspired by Hope.*

Zero in on these three areas a little more. What three words in these verses are also found in 1 Corinthians 13:13? Give an explanation for their use in these verses:

1. *Faith*

2. *Hope*

TRAINING FOR THE PRIZE

3. _Love & love being the greatest._

Challenge question: What is the difference between work and labor? Why is it important in this verse?

Paul encouraged the church at Thessalonica to train themselves in Jesus' truth and teaching. In verses 4–10, can you find other training guidelines Paul shared with his brothers and sisters in Christ?

Hidden Treasures

After studying 1 Thessalonians 1 and reviewing "Real Life Facts," give examples of the ways spiritual training is like physical training.

warn the idle - encourage timid - help weak - be patient - kind - joyful & stay in state of prayer

Celebrating Treasured Gifts

Get real with God right now. Are you training for the "prize"? Are you doing what it takes to live a life sold out to Jesus? Are you exercising your prayer life to increase your heart capacity for Jesus? Are you working out with the Lord daily through reading His Word? Use this time to go to the Father in prayer as you journal your thoughts. Take a deep breath, and get up, get out, and get going!

Reflection Pause

How does regular exercise benefit your ability to breathe? As you exercise on a regular basis, your lung capacity increases, allowing a larger volume of air to enter your lungs. High intensity workouts require deep breathing, which in turn causes the lungs to increase air intake. This is beneficial for everyone because an increased lung capacity not only enhances your stamina level, but also it is good for your overall health. A larger lung capacity and increased oxygen levels help circulate blood in your body. A better blood flow aids in cleansing the veins and arteries.

Wow—increased lung capacity = increased oxygen intake = increased blood flow = blood and vein cleansing!

How does spiritual exercise benefit your spiritual breathing? By now you know I love to use real life lessons as a way to teach a spiritual truth. So here goes. As long as you are alive, you are breathing air; and we know that there are ways to improve your breathing capacity. You can do the same with your spiritual breathing. The more time you spend with Jesus, the more you enhance your intake of the Holy Spirit. The minute you become alive in Christ, the Holy Spirit resides inside you forever. But as you desire to live a life sold out to Jesus—walking in the Spirit and not in the flesh—you increase your spiritual lung capacity. The deeper you breathe in the Holy Spirit, the more you allow Him to flow through you. He cleanses your life of impurities. As you breathe Him in, you experience the fulfillment of His presence. He gives you the yearning to exercise your prayer life with Him, stay fit in your Bible study, and work out your daily problems through Him.

Wow—increased time with Jesus = increased spiritual understanding = increased Holy Spirit flow = spiritual cleansing!

WEEK 9: DAY 2

ENDURING THE RACE

Everyone who competes in the games goes into strict training. They do it to get a crown that will not last; but we do it to get a crown that will last forever.

—1 Corinthians 9:25

One lap left! I'm not sure I will make it!
You've been training for a year, but in the middle of the race you're beginning to doubt yourself. At this point, you are not sure you've prepared enough.

I can't do it. My legs are giving out.

Quitting seems the only option. As you begin to slow down, you look over at the sideline. You see a friend jumping up and down with her hands raised to the sky, cheering you on to the finish line. All of a sudden, something happens. Adrenaline kicks in, and you pick up your pace.

I am not giving up. I am finishing strong!

Before you know it, you cross the finish line. As you collapse to the ground, you feel a sense of accomplishment. You realize your friend's encouragement spurred you forward to complete the race.

Doesn't the same thing happen in our Christian lives? We study God's Word, and we pray and worship Him. This groundwork is what we need to stay strong in our walk with Jesus. This preparation gives us a solid foundation so that when this life race gets tough, we can endure. As Christian sisters and brothers we are called to encourage one another in our daily walks with the Lord.

Do you realize that after this week we just have one lap left in this study? Persist to the end, sweet sister. I have my hands up in the air, cheering you on to the finish line. Feel the adrenaline rush into your heart as you continue forward. The Lord is applauding your commitment and smiling at your efforts. As 1 Corinthians 9:25 says, we are in "strict training." Let's not waste another minute. Have fun today "Enduring the Race"!

Scripture Excavation

Our Scripture focus today is 1 Thessalonians 2. Please read the entire chapter at one time to get an overall picture. Keep in mind that Paul was writing to the new converts at the church in Thessalonica. Those new believers needed a deeper understanding of the Scriptures, true doctrine, and application.

A thriving and busy port, Thessalonica served as a major trade route and thoroughfare. It was the largest city in Macedonia and was the capital. Paul took advantage of the city's dynamics to spread the gospel message. As a result, a large number of people accepted Paul's message of salvation through Jesus. (Don't forget our theme for the week: "Fit for Jesus.")

Write a summary of 1 Thessalonians 2, including the purpose, highlights, and focus of the chapter.

presenting God's message of salvation - encouraged - focus on God's return

Do you see a verse where Paul encouraged the believers? If so, how would this have spurred them forward in their knowledge of and faith in Jesus?

★ 2:12 live in such a way that would be worthy of God

Why do you think Paul said, "Like a mother caring for her little children," in verse 7 and, "as a father deals with his own children," in verse 11? How would these two relationships encourage new believers to stay strong in their faith?

They can understand this love & protection - encouragement comes from imagining the depth of God's love for us -

Look at verse 12. Why is this verse significant to our study today?

live in the way that would be worthy of God - what do people think of God from watching you?

ENDURING THE RACE

Hidden Treasures

Let's do a comparison study between "Enduring the Race" and 1 Thessalonians 2. Where did Paul hint of the struggles in his life? In your opinion, what was Paul's purpose in sharing this with the believers?

2:13 - Suffered for countrymen -- Jews who killed Jesus

In verses 13–16, Paul reminded the new Thessalonian believers of their own struggles. This is very important: what was Paul's purpose for strengthening these believers' resolve, and why did he remind them of their conflicts?

Celebrating Treasured Gifts

"Everyone who competes in the games goes into strict training. They do it to get a crown that will not last; but we do it to get a crown that will last forever" (1 Cor. 9:25). Praise God for all He is teaching you. Give Him the glory for His encouragement along the way. Thank Him for the times in your life when your faith was strengthened through trials and struggles. If you are experiencing difficult times right now, try this approach: Praise God and thank Him for what you can see He is doing through the struggle. Praise God for your trials. He loves to hear us sing His praises!

Reflection Pause

Endurance means having the necessary stamina to complete a task. It requires patience and staying power. A marathon runner might be born with the ability to run long distances, but this natural gift doesn't mean he or she is automatically able to run twenty-six miles. It takes time to strengthen his or her muscles and lung capacity. He or she begins by running short distances and, over time, builds up endurance to run farther and farther. This slow training process gives the runner an aptitude for resilience during the race's difficult moments.

As a Christian, the minute you accept Jesus into your life you are given the ability to develop your relationship with Him, but it takes time and steadfastness to deepen your walk with Him. It is like training for a marathon. To stay strong throughout the race, you need to build your staying power ahead of time. Spending time in the Word and in prayer develops faith and trust. The more you work out under the master Trainer, the more refined your spiritual strength. And as a result, "Reflecting Him" becomes automatic!

    Stay steady in your spiritual workouts. Train for the long distances. Realize God allows you to break a sweat sometimes during your spiritual training. This should give you a stronger faith and the necessary strength to endure the test of time. Remember, Jesus is cheering for you. Your other sisters and brothers in Christ are cheering for you as well!

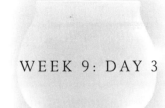

WEEK 9: DAY 3

STRENGTH TRAINING

For now we really live, since you are standing firm in the Lord.

—1 Thessalonians 3:8

Some people are naturally born with a muscled body. The moment my second son entered the world, the doctor said, "Look at the muscles on this baby boy!" Yet others are born with rolls of plumpness for baby protection. Why are we given certain muscle characteristics? One thing is certain: we all have the ability to strengthen our muscles. Our diets also affect our body and muscle potential. The foods we eat provide the nutrients our bodies need to grow and develop properly.

Exercise also affects muscle tone and power. My husband worked in remote areas of Africa where ninety percent of the native diet was from some kind of root. This limited food source restricted the people's growth patterns. The men in this area refrained from manual labor and got little exercise, so they tended to be smaller in stature and had little muscle strength.

Today we focus on strength training and how it affects the whole body. We will compare this to the spiritual strength training God provides His children.

Scripture Excavation

We are making progress through 1 Thessalonians. Take a few minutes and read the entire third chapter. Let your heart absorb what Paul said to the new believers. Write a summary of this chapter by breaking it into three different sections and giving each a heading.

- Section 1: _____

    Heading: _____

    Summary: _____

    _____

    _____

    _____

- Section 2: _____

    Heading: _____

    Summary: _____

    _____

    _____

    _____

- Section 3: _____

    Heading: _____

    Summary: _____

    _____

    _____

    _____

STRENGTH TRAINING

Whom did God send to strengthen and encourage the church at Thessalonica? Why do you think Paul sent this person? Who benefited from his encouragement?

_____
_____

Where and how was Paul strengthened in this chapter? How can making godly choices encourage other believers?

_____
_____

Hidden Treasures

What is stunting your spiritual growth? Maybe your focus in life is on material things, such as trendy clothes or a new house. Are you more concerned with peer approval than with God? Does this affect your spiritual strength training routine? Confess to the Lord the areas that are diminishing your walk with Him. Proclaim to God ways in which you want to change.

_____
_____

Celebrating Treasured Gifts

Praise God for the forgiveness He freely offers His children. Praise Him for His grace and mercy, which goes beyond our understanding. Write a prayer of praise based on our focus verse for the day: "For now we really live, since you are standing firm in the Lord" (1 Thess. 3:8).

_____
_____
_____
_____
_____

Reflection Pause

I want you to grasp something very important. You just went through some exercises on spiritual strength training. Think about this: For a weightlifter to develop stronger muscles, he first must break down his muscles by lifting heavier weights to tire his muscles. For a Christian to gain a stronger understanding of God's Word, he must break down the Scriptures by spending time and energy with God. Keep it up! God is showing you incredible things about Himself and how to live out the Christian life. Are you starting to see how God regularly provides spiritual life lessons? Continue to ask the Holy Spirit to help you to be aware of these spiritual truths in your everyday life.

WEEK 9: DAY 4

TEAM BUILDING

Now about brotherly love we do not need to write to you, for you yourselves have been taught by God to love each other.

—1 Thessalonians 4:9

Can I count on her? Is she going to follow through this time?
This team has experienced ups and downs due to one person's lack of commitment.
She hasn't been at practice to learn the drills, but she thinks she knows it all.
Frustrated. Bewildered. It all comes down to this last game.
Maybe she is naturally gifted and doesn't need as much practice as the others. But a win can't be based on one team member's talent. It must be the whole team.

Leading this team to a winning season is furthest from your mind. As the coach, you feel defeated. But it is team failure—to put it lightly.

I can feel the animosity and hostility from the other girls. The looks thrown her way on the court could kill. I must pull them all together! They need this life lesson much more than a district title.

What do you think the coach needs to do to build a dream team? How can her actions and coaching influence the team? An excellent coach is one who knows how to teach a team to rely on one another, to build up the team rather than tear it down, and to inspire the girls to give their all. Today we focus our attention on team building from a spiritual perspective. Enjoy the journey!

Scripture Excavation

We are moving into 1 Thessalonians 4. As you did in the previous days, read the chapter. This gives you an overall view of its meaning. Let's do some more spiritual strength building. Break this chapter into three parts and give each a heading.

- Section 1: _____

    Heading: _____

    Summary: _____

    _____

    _____

- Section 2: _____

    Heading: _____

    Summary: _____

    _____

    _____

- Section 3: _____

    Heading: _____

    Summary: _____

    _____

    _____

TEAM BUILDING

Do you see a change in Paul's tone? If so, where and why?
_____
_____

Where did Paul begin to rally the team together? What did He ask of them?
_____
_____

Hidden Treasures

Can you think of some comparisons between coaching a sports team and building a spiritual team for the Lord—such as a family, committee at church, Bible study, ministry, etc.? Where does good leadership begin? Take note of Paul's leadership qualities and skills. Use references from 1 Thessalonians 4.
_____
_____

Remember our story at the beginning of the day? Answer the following questions based on that short story: What do you think the coach needs to do to build the dream team? How can her actions and coaching influence the team?
_____
_____

Finally, I want you to focus on 1 Thessalonians 4:16–18. Imagine this dream team meeting in the clouds. Describe this experience. Be creative, and reference any other verses you think of.
_____
_____

Celebrating Treasured Gifts

Use this time to be real with the Lord. Think of teams with which you are involved either as a coach or a teammate—family, church, ministry, work, committees, youth group, children's club, etc. Are you giving your all? Are you leading with encouragement? Are you praying for and with your teammates? Are you connecting with your team members? What's so exciting is that God called all believers to be part of His dream team! What a gift and a blessing to behold!
_____
_____
_____

Reflection Pause

In the quiet of your heart, can you hear the orchestra's music? Do you hear each instrument's individual sounds? Many times when played alone, they might sound out of tune or off key. But when blended together, they make a beautiful noise, each one complementing the other. The music is inspiring, soothing, and even mesmerizing. "They all continued with one accord in prayer" (Acts 1:14 NKJV).

In the verse above, the Greek word for "accord" is *homothumadon,* which means "one mind, one passion."[17] This is actually a combination of two words meaning to "rush along" and "in unison." Like an orchestra, each note played at the same time is different but harmonizes in pitch and tone, captivating an audience from the moment the first note is played.

This is the picture of the body of Christ when we are of one mind. Like instruments of a famous orchestra directed by a concertmaster, the Holy Spirit blends together the saints' prayers. God desires for His children to pray together as a team so they make beautiful music through their prayers. The believers in Acts knew the importance of coming together to lift their praises and requests to the Lord. We should live out their example in our own lives.

Why do we make corporate prayer a last resort? Over and over, God's Word shows us examples of believers praying together as a team and God answering. God calls us to pray! This is exciting—God gives us an opportunity to participate in eternity with Him through prayer. Let's do it! Let's pray together! Don't miss the blessing of drawing nearer to God and other brothers and sisters in Christ as you create beautiful "prayer" songs together.

WEEK 9: DAY 5

FINAL INSTRUCTIONS

Be joyful always; pray continually; give thanks in all circumstances, for this is God's will for you in Christ Jesus.

—1 Thessalonians 5:16–18

Her entire body shakes as she makes her way to the starting block. She keeps wiping her hands on her swimsuit and is having trouble getting her goggles set. You've never seen your daughter this nervous. All you know to do is pray—like never before.

The swim coach gives his final instructions. It appears as if his gentle words calmed her a bit. Now a look of determination has replaced her appearance of panic. What did he say to her? What helped her turn the focus from fear of failure to an "I can do it" attitude? As a coach, it is his job to be there for the final instructions. He guides and directs the athlete until the whistle blows.

REFLECTING HIM

The same holds true in Christianity. Jesus constantly guides and directs us. He is the head coach with the "final instructions." Our role is to be teachable, easy to coach, and ready to take instructions at any moment. The more we keep our eyes on Him, the more we understand His coaching. Sometimes Jesus uses assistant coaches to help us in the game of life. Paul was one of the best assistant coaches ever.

Today as you move through the last chapter of Thessalonians, notice His incredible ability to spur the team forward. Have fun learning from Paul, a great instructor.

Scripture Excavation

Paul gave us a great list of final instructions in 1 Thessalonians 5. For this last chapter, we are going to make a play list. This is an instruction guide on the way Jesus desires us to play the real game of life. Read 1 Thessalonians 5. Then fill in the list of things a Christian should and should not do.

Final Instructions for Believers	Do	Don't Do

What did you learn from this list? How did it encourage you?

_____

_____

Circle the "do" that you find the most difficult to accomplish. Circle the "don't do" that is the most difficult to abolish from your life. Take time right now to pray over this list, asking the Lord to help you.

_____

_____

Write the verse or block of verses from chapter 5 that encourage(s) you to surrender these areas to the Lord.

_____

_____

Hidden Treasures

There is a block of verses hidden within the depths of 1 Thessalonians 5 that represents the heart of Paul's whole message to believers. It is a short series of commands planted in the middle of all these do's and don'ts.

OK, I will tell you. Read verses 16–18. As we end our day with these final instructions, think about the value of each one. They are priceless! Explain each of these commands:

FINAL INSTRUCTIONS

- "Be joyful always."

_____

_____

- "Pray continually."

_____

_____

- "Give thanks in all circumstances."

_____

_____

Celebrating Treasured Gifts

Take time to write a praise prayer to the Lord. Thank Him for His final instructions. His Word is all we need.

_____

_____

_____

_____

_____

_____

Reflection Pause

Take a moment to reflect again on 1 Thessalonians 5:16–18. Notice how this block of scriptures ends: "For this is God's will for you in Christ Jesus." How powerful! How encouraging! To be joyful does not always mean being happy. Happiness is a feeling. We could experience a difficult circumstance and certainly not "feel" happy about it. But if we take this verse to heart and apply it to our lives, we see the situation as a time of growing in our faith. It encourages us to get on our knees and thank God for what He is doing despite our circumstances, because it is God's will for us in Christ Jesus. The blessing of God's Final Instruction Booklet—His Word—is all we need to live a life sold out to Jesus. The final result? To become His reflection!

WEEK 10

SO . . . REFLECT HIM: LOVE GOD, LIVE FOR JESUS, BREATHE IN THE HOLY SPIRIT

And we, who with unveiled faces all reflect the Lord's glory, are being transformed into his likeness with ever-increasing glory, which comes from the Lord, who is the Spirit.

—2 Corinthians 3:18

Hurray! Congratulations! You did it. Did you ever doubt you would finish this Bible study? Did you encounter any hurdles? As we journeyed together through the pages of this Bible study, God allowed us to experience Him. Through these treasured moments He transformed us into more of Christ's likeness. Seeking to know Jesus is God's heart's cry for His children. When we have a willingness to be changed, God can do amazing things in our lives. He wants each believer to reflect Him—at home, with our families, at work, at the grocery store, driving in traffic, during difficult times, at church, and at all other times. In other words, twenty-four hours a day, seven days a week. Why? Because God calls believers to spread Jesus' message to the world.

We are to leave a legacy for our children and their children. As we reflect Jesus, our kids desire to mirror Him the same way. I am not talking about passing on a religion, but a relationship with Jesus. "One generation shall praise Your works to another, and shall declare Your mighty acts" (Ps. 145:4 NKJV).

Have you experienced a family reunion? I don't mean a gathering that just involves your parents, brothers, sisters, and their children, but one that extends to the previous generations two- and threefold. Each summer, our family is blessed to attend the annual Lucas Family Reunion, which has taken place for about fifty-five years. This year, as I mingled with the more than one hundred relatives in attendance, I realized how many believers are in my family lineage. In my great-great-grandfather's family there were seventeen sons and one daughter. Can you imagine the food their mama prepared on a daily basis? Think about all the clothes washed by hand on a scrub board! Come to find out, these eighteen children were consistently taught God's Word by their parents. All of a sudden, this verse popped into my mind: "One generation shall praise Your works to another, and shall declare Your mighty acts."

As we gathered on Saturday evening to sing, the harmony of "Amazing Grace" echoed through the retreat camp. At that moment, I realized that I am a product of the generations before me who loved Jesus with all their hearts. Chill bumps covered my whole body! I wondered about the prayers my ancestors prayed years and years ago. Did my great-great-great-grandmother ask the Lord to capture the hearts of her offspring's children for generations to come? Are these prayers still coming to fruition today? As tears welled up in my eyes, I thanked the Lord for my family.

A personal conviction instantly enveloped me: God is calling me to pass on this same truth to my children and their children and so on. I realized that the more I seek to be like Jesus, the more I will reflect Him—and that, in turn, affects my offspring. Also, learning and applying His Word influences them to do the same. Prayer is a key component for passing on Jesus' message to our heirs. I diligently started praying for my kids to marry the person God already has chosen for each of them. Because of their parents' bond with each other and God, my children's children will be encouraged to love Jesus. This thought spurred me forward to pray for my grandchildren (I am not a grandmother yet, but one day) to become mighty men and women for God's kingdom. Then this thought came to my heart: *Once I am in heaven with Jesus, the only way I can affect the generations in my family is through the prayers prayed while I was still here on earth!* We see this over and over in the Old Testament where God's promise to an individual is fulfilled in succeeding generations. *Reflecting Him* now is the way to pass on the message to the next generation.

Completing this Bible study—*Reflecting Him*—should have helped you embed His lessons in your heart. Now, take time to look back at each week of the study and answer a few questions. This will be a great review, so have fun finishing this last week of the study!

Week 1: Reflections in Life

Where were you in your walk with Christ when you started this study?

_____

_____

What did you want to accomplish by the end of this study?

_____

_____

SO . . . REFLECT HIM: LOVE GOD, LIVE FOR JESUS, BREATHE IN THE HOLY SPIRIT

Do you see yourself differently after completing this study? How?
_____
_____

Week 2: Created for God, by God

What impacted you the most as you studied that week's lessons?
_____
_____

What did you learn from comparing the pottery process to the Christian life?
_____
_____

Week 3: Senses of the Soul

What life lesson did you learn from studying the human sensory system (touch, taste, aroma, hearing, sight)?
_____
_____

Which day meant the most to you in Week 3?
_____
_____

Week 4: The Power Source

After reviewing this week, what new concept did you learn?
_____
_____

Discuss the daily lesson that meant the most to you in Week 4.
_____
_____

Week 5: Prayer from the Inside Out

How was your prayer life encouraged through Week 5's lessons? Have you experienced any changes? If so, explain.

_____
_____

What concept meant the most to you from that week?

_____
_____

Week 6: Prayer Fuels Faith

Looking back at Week 6, did God reveal any new concepts as you compared the gasoline supply chain to having faith in Him? Explain your answer.

_____
_____

How has your faith grown since studying Week 6? Do you have a real life faith story to share?

_____
_____

Week 7: The Control Syndrome

What did you learn when you compared gardening to the way God wants to stimulate your growth as a Christian?

_____
_____

Which day meant the most to you and why?

_____
_____

Week 8: Roadblocks Ahead

What did God reveal to you in Week 8 that will remain in your heart forever?

_____
_____

SO . . . REFLECT HIM: LOVE GOD, LIVE FOR JESUS, BREATHE IN THE HOLY SPIRIT

How do you view the detours and diversions in your life after working your way through this week?

_____

_____

Week 9: Fit for Jesus

How has Week 9 influenced your thoughts on living a life sold out to Jesus?

_____

_____

Write one thing you learned when you compared fitness and exercise to Paul's teaching in 1 Thessalonians.

_____

_____

Oh, sister-friend, please continue to seek the Lord through other Bible studies. Jesus desires for you to call on Him daily. He is waiting for you twenty-four hours a day, seven days a week. Look for Him throughout your day. He continually gives you opportunities to see His influence on your life. Ask the Holy Spirit to help you be aware of God at work in everyday situations.

Thank you from the bottom of my heart for committing to this Bible study, *Reflecting Him*. Writing this study is an experience I never will forget. My little Maltese served as my companion through these months of writing. If she could talk she would share a number of stories with you. I remember one time when the Lord showed me something brand new—I got so excited that I jumped out of my chair and exclaimed, "God, You are so much fun!" Shaking profusely, my little dog ran as fast as she could and hid under the bed. She didn't come out for the rest of the day.

I encourage you to dive headfirst into your relationship with Jesus. Exclaim in your own words, "God, You are so much fun!" The more you seek Him, the more you will begin *Reflecting Him*. As you reflect Him, you find yourself *Living for Jesus and Loving It!*

From my heart to yours,
Carla McDougal

BIBLIOGRAPHY

Strong, James, LL.D, S.T.D., *The Strong's Exhaustive Concordance of the Bible*, Peabody: Hendrickson, 1986.

Web sites

10 Tips for Driving in Work Zones. US Department of Transportation Federal Highway Administration. Retrieved November 10, 2009, from http://safety.fhwa.dot.gov/wz/wz_awareness/2008/factsht08.cfm.

Amazing Facts About the Human Body—The Respiratory System. Gunther von Hagens. Retrieved December 29, 2009, from http://www.docstoc.com/docs/2290519/Amazing-Facts-About-the-Human-Body.

Amazing Facts About the Skin. Retrieved December 28, 2009, from http://health.learninginfo.org/skin-facts.htm.

Amazing Facts About Your Amazing Eye. Babyspyro. Retrieved April 14, 2009, from http://purpleslinky.com/trivia/science/amazing-facts-about-your-amazing-eyes.

Companion Planting. Homestead Harvest. Retrieved October 15, 2009, from http://www.homesteadharvest.com/companion-planting-html.

Detour. Retrieved December 29, 2009, from http://www.thefreedictionary.com/detour.

The Mouth and Digestion. Retrieved September 3, 2009, from http://www.funtrivia.com/en/subtopics/The-Mouth-and-Digestion-166774.html.

Sun. Retrieved July 20, 2009, from http://www.nasa.gov/worldbook/sun_worldbook.html.

Vegetable and Fruit Pest and Beneficial Insect Profile. Retrieved October 15, 2009, from http://www.vegedge.umn.edu/vegpest/pests.htm.

ENDNOTES

1. James Strong, S.T.D., LL.D, *Strong's Exhaustive Concordance of the Bible* (Peabody, MA: Hendrickson Publishers, 1986).
2. James Strong, S.T.D., LL.D, *Strong's Exhaustive Concordance of the Bible* (Peabody, MA: Hendrickson Publishers, 1986).
3. James Strong, S.T.D., LL.D, *Strong's Exhaustive Concordance of the Bible* (Peabody, MA: Hendrickson Publishers, 1986).
4. James Strong, S.T.D., LL.D, *Strong's Exhaustive Concordance of the Bible* (Peabody, MA: Hendrickson Publishers, 1986).
5. James Strong, S.T.D., LL.D, *Strong's Exhaustive Concordance of the Bible* (Peabody, MA: Hendrickson Publishers, 1986).
6. "Amazing Facts About Your Amazing Eyes," *Science*, http://purpleslinky.com/trivia/science/amazing-facts-about-your-amazing-eyes. Accessed April 14, 2009.
7. A 2 Z of Health, Beauty, and Fitness, "Amazing Facts about the Skin," *A 2 Z of Health, Beauty, and Fitness*, http://health.learninginfo.org/skin-facts.htm. Accessed December 28, 2009.
8. FunTrivia.com, "The Mouth and Digestion," *FunTrivia.com*, http://www.funtrivia.com/en/subtopics/The-Mouth-and-Digestion-166774.html. Accessed September 3, 2009.
9. Docstoc.com, "Amazing Facts about the Human Body—The Respiratory System," *Body Worlds 4 Press Office*, http://www.docstoc.com/docs/2290519/Amazing-Facts-About-the-Human-Body. Accessed December 29, 2009.
10. James Strong, S.T.D., LL.D, *Strong's Exhaustive Concordance of the Bible* (Peabody, MA: Hendrickson Publishers, 1986).
11. NASA, "Sun," *World Book at NASA*, http://www.nasa.gov/worldbook/sun_worldbook.html. Accessed July 20, 2009.
12. College of Food, Agriculture, and Natural Resource Science, "Vegetable & Fruit Pest and Beneficial Insect Profiles," University of Minnesota, http://www.vegedge.umn.edu/vegpest/pests.htm. Accessed October 15, 2009.

13. Homestead Harvest, "Companion Planting," http://www.homesteadharvest.com/companion-planting.html. Accessed October 15, 2009.
14. James Strong, S.T.D., LL.D, *Strong's Exhaustive Concordance of the Bible* (Peabody, MA: Hendrickson Publishers, 1986).
15. The Free Dictionary, "Detour," http://www.thefreedictionary.com/detour. Accessed December 29, 2009.
16. FHWA, "10 Tips for Driving in Work Zones," *Work Zone Safety and Mobility Fact Sheet*, http://safety.fhwa.dot.gov/wz/wz_awareness/2008/factsht08.cfm. Accessed November 10, 2009.
17. James Strong, S.T.D., LL.D, *Strong's Exhaustive Concordance of the Bible* (Peabody, MA: Hendrickson Publishers, 1986).

To order additional copies of this book call:
1-877-421-READ (7323)
or please visit our Web site at
www.winepressbooks.com

If you enjoyed this quality custom-published book,
drop by our Web site for more books and information.

www.winepressgroup.com
"Your partner in custom publishing."

Ladies Retreat - $40.00
La Salle Hotel -
Bryan - Friday - Saturday

Celina - Day Care - Church